Linda Hasselstrom

Dakota   Bones

Dakota Bones

Collected Poems

of

Linda Hasselstrom

Spoon River Poetry Press
1993

For my father
John Hasselstrom
July 8, 1909-August 7, 1992

Published by Spoon River Poetry Press, David Pichaske editor, Box 6, Granite Falls Minnesota 56241.
Typesetting by Kristin Pichaske.
Printing by Thomson and Shore, Dexter, Michigan.
Cover photograph by Jeff Jacobson.

ISBN 0-944024-23-8

2   3   4   5

CONTENTS

VIII

Preface

My first book, *Caught by One Wing*, was published in a letterpress edition of 500 copies in 1984. Julie Holcomb handset the type and created a signed and numbered edition of "Mulch" in her shop behind Browser Books in San Francisco. The book and the broadside were beautiful and too fragile and expensive for the rough handling books get in shipment and on display in bookstores.

In 1987, Dave Pichaske published *Roadkill*, my second poetry collection, through his Spoon River Poetry Press in Peoria, Illinios. By 1990, the demand for *Roadkill* encouraged him to reprint *Caught by One Wing* as well. He photographed the original pages, provided a new cover—his picture of a hayfield near my house—and a lower price. By then, Spoon River was in Granite Falls, Minnesota.

By 1992, I had published three nonfiction titles, including *Windbreak*, a journal of a year on the ranch; *Going Over East*, essays; and *Land Circle*, a blend of poetry and essays.

This new collection includes about thirty pages of new poems, as well as the complete texts of both *Caught by One Wing* and *Roadkill*; we've corrected typographical errors, but the texts of both books are complete in this edition. An alphabetized index appears at the back of the book.

Naturally, nearly ten years after publication of those early poems, my writing has changed, as have some of my views; I've learned more about poetry. Certainly newer poems differ from older ones. "No honest poet," said T.S. Eliot, "can ever feel quite sure of the permanent value of what he has written: he may have wasted his time and messed up his life for nothing."

However, I've chosen not to revise or delete even poems I consider inferior and wish I hadn't published. In 1984, I was forty-one years old; I'd been writing for thirty-two years, and didn't know if I'd ever see my name on the spine of a book. When Julie Holcomb suggested publishing my poetry, I thought it might be the only book I'd ever produce, and included some poems for personal, nostalgic reasons. If certain of those poems had never appeared in print, they wouldn't be here.

But to change published work would be to edit the self and the writer I was then in the light of what I know now. In ten more years, I might do it again; by the time I die, it might appear I'd never written a truly horrible poem, or that writing is a seamless process, a matter of talent alone, without struggle, without development. New writers deserve to know that learning to write well is a slow, laborious maturation; Mary Heaton Vorse called it "the art of applying the seat of the pants to the seat of the chair." Practice can improve a writer who begins badly, but readers may never see bad, early poems by fine poets unless they doggedly search out early periodical publications. As a teacher of new writers of all ages, I've declared that practice can improve anyone's writing, so I can't hide my failures. Like most writers, I admit rewriting some poems between magazine publication and a later book.

Challenge to new writers: find poems that show awkwardness, less skill than others; analyze how you—or I—might rewrite them now. Compare them to your own. Every poem (or story or essay) a writer reads becomes part of that day's lesson in writing. With Stephen Leacock, "I'm a great believer in luck. I find the harder I work, the more I have of it."

LH, 1992

I

"I have picked flowers where I found them—have picked up sea shells and rocks and pieces of wood where there were sea shells and rocks and pieces of wood that I liked. . . . When I found the beautiful white bones on the desert I picked them up and took them home too. . . . I have used these things to say what is to me the wideness and wonder of the world as I live in it . . . when I started painting the pelvis bones I was most interested in the holes in the bones—what I saw through them—particularly the blue from holding them up in the sun against the sky as one is apt to do when one seems to have more sky than earth in one's world."

—*Georgia O'Keeffe*

Staying In One Place

Riding fence last summer
I saw a meadowlark caught by one wing.
(My father saw one caught so, once;
in freeing it, taught me compassion.)
                              He'd flown
futile circles around the wire, snapping bones.
Head folded on yellow breast,
he hung by one sinew, dead.

Gathering cattle in the fall
I rode that way again;
his yellow breast was bright as autumn air
or his own song.

I'm snowed in now, only a path
from the house to the cows in the corral.
Miles away he still hangs,
frost in his eyesockets
swinging in the wind.

I lie heavy in my bed alone, turning, turning,
seeing the house layered in drifts of snow
and dust and years and scraps of empty paper.
He should be light, light
bone and snowflake light.

Bone

I am a saguaro, ribs thrust gray
against blue hot sky.
                        I am
a polished jawbone, teeth white
against the grass.
I have become all that I see:
an elegant bone gnawed clean,
leaving only bone the end,

bone the beginning,
bone the skyline mountain.

Spring

Spring is here:
the first skunk lies dead
at the highway's rim,
white fur still bright,
nose stained with one drop of blood.

A calf born dead yesterday
was found by coyotes in the night:
only the head and one front foot remain.
The cat preens in a pile of meadowlark feathers.
A blue jay is eating baby robins.
The hens caught a mouse in their corn
this morning; pecked it to shrieking shreds.

It's spring;
time to kill the kittens.
Their mewing blends with the meadowlark song.
I tried drowning them once;
it was slow, painful.
Now I bash each with a wrench,
once, hard.

Each death makes a dull sound,
going deep in the ground
without
reverberations.

Mulch

A mulch is a layer of organic matter
used to control weeds,
preserve moisture,
and improve the fertility of the soil.
You will not find naked soil
in the wilderness.

I started cautiously: newspapers,
hay, a few magazines;
Robert Redford stared up
between the rhubarb and the lettuce.

Then one day, cleaning shelves,
I found some old love letters.
I've always burned them, for the symbolism.
But the ashes, gray and dusty as old passions,
would blow about the yard for days
stinging my eyes,
bitter on my tongue.

So I mulched them:
gave undying love to the tomatoes,
the memory of your gentle hands to the squash.
It seemed to do them good,
and it taught me a whole new style
of gardening.

Now my garden is the best in the wilderness,
and I mulch everything:
bills; check stubs;
dead kittens and baby chicks.
I seldom answer letters; I mulch them
with the plans I made for children of my own,
photographs of places I've been
and a husband I had once;
as well as old bouquets
and an occasional unsatisfactory lover.

Nothing is wasted.

Strange plants push up among the corn,
leaves heavy with dark water,
but there are
no weeds.

Deer

        —for George

They must be out there, in the gray
sagebrush between this rough highway
and the shining, white-topped Bighorns.
I only see them exploded
by speeding trucks. A little hoof
on a bloody leg waves at me
from a mess in the other lane.

This morning, love, we saw thirteen
ghostly does and fawns, one big buck,
go dancing in the blue dawn haze
among trees and sly alfalfa.

7

Seasons in South Dakota

—for Rodney, who asked

I

Dirty snow left in the gullies, pale
green spread overnight on the hills
mark spring.
                    Taking corn to the hens
I hear a waterfall of redwing blackbird song.
When I open the windows to their raucous mating
I let in something else as well:
soon I'll pace the hills under the moon.

II

Watching struggling heifers birth,
greasing the tractor, I may miss
summer.
                    Like spring, it bursts open:
blooming hay demands the mower.
All day I ride the tractor,
isolated by roar.
it's time to turn the bulls out
to the cows, check leaning fences.
Even in summer nights' sweat
I hate to sleep alone.
When I'm too tired to care,
I still hear the larks, feel
the cold flow in each window at dawn.

III

Autumn whistles in some day when I'm
riding the gray gelding
bringing in fat calves for sale:
the air quick-chills, grass turns brown.
Last fall I found two gray hairs;
just as quick, winter came:

I was hurrying to pile fresh wood
from the one-woman crosscut saw
when the first flakes crowded the sky.

IV

Despite the feeding, pitching hay to
black cows with frost-rimmed eyes,
cutting ice on the dam under the eyes
of sky and one antelope,
there's still time to sit before the fire,
curse the dead cold outside,
the other empty chair.

Grandmother

I always see her hands first, turning
the handle of the Foley food mill.
The veins are knotted over old bones;
spicy tomato steam rises around
her white hair. A worn gold ring turns on
her finger but never will slide off
over the knuckle. Solid as a
young woman, she grew thin, forgot our
names. Hands that fed four daughters lay still.
She left us little: brown unlabeled pictures,
a dozen crocheted afghans, piles of patched jeans.
In the cellar, crowded shelves bear jars of beans,
peas, corn, meat.
Labels like white silent mouths
open and close in the dark.

Memorial Day

I'm on the hill above the town, with
buffalo grass and graves. Nothing else
grows here. These thrive, deep-rooted, pulling
some thin life from the thick clay soil.

Propriety demands the sod turn
once a year above these ancestors.
They're just bones to me. I'd rather let
buffalo grass grow. There's alfalfa
on Charley Hasselstrom's mound; he'd like
that, says my father, his son.
He worked all his life to grow the stuff,
mow it, stack it, feed it to his cows;
worried about it getting hailed out,
burned out, eaten up by grasshoppers.
Now I have to turn under six plants
that volunteered for him.

Dust blooms below the hill: another makes
the yearly journey. I'll leave the spade
against Martha's rock, try the hoe, hack
at the stubborn roots worked deep in clay.
The shock moves up my arm, down the hoe,
drumming to bones I'll never see, deep
in the earth, deep inside my flesh.

When My Father Waters His Trees

                                    he puts the hose
in the fifty-gallon drum, stands in the shade till
it's full. Doorless, the green '49 Chevy truck
grates, starts, lumbers out of the yard. The running boards,
still black, snap; the jack rattles; the windshield wiper
on the floor bounces left and right. One fender is
beginning to sag but the boards in the box are
new oak. The glove box is wired shut and contains one
pair of wire clippers and a cigarette pack
put there in 1956 when dad stopped smoking.

                                       My father says
the green truck starts when it's too cold
for the new one. He pulls up to the tree row, dips
a bucket out, pours it on the first tree, slowly
walks back for another, arms swinging. It's evening,
he's been haying all day; he fills and then empties
the drum several times, waits for a late supper.

                             Sometimes
I hear the old truck start just before dawn,
while it's cool. On last year's birthday I heard him say,
"Well , I'm 69. Shall I quit, or should I plant
more trees?"
                 He got twenty cedar from the Forest Service,
took his long-handled spade out northeast of the house.
Most of the shoots are a foot high now, growing green.

Digging Potatoes

I

We divided it all, but
my grandmother's shoes wouldn't fit
anyone but me.
                    She'd walked years
to the old stove with firewood,
to the chickenhouse for eggs,
to the pasture to check the cows.

II

We buried her in the fall, dry
grasses blowing on the hilltop.
There were no leaves to rustle; no trees
can grow on that dry hill. The view is clear
to the river, the gumbo hills beyond.
                              We even
divided the bright spring flowers—
the hothouse roses, carnations—that
blanketed her coffin. I dropped a rosebud
as if by accident.

III

Wearing her shoes, I'm digging potatoes.
The sweet, rotten earth smell reaches up;
soil clings to my fingers, to the red
potatoes I drop in the bucket. I expect
to see her face at the bottom of each hole,
hear her voice answering the question
I've barely begun to ask.

Blackbirds

        —for Tom

I

In spring, redwing blackbirds are the first back,
raucous clouds in the trees,
gold-rimmed red wings sparkling,
inundating the prairie
in waterfalls of sound.

II

When the tractor chugs into the field in June,
mowing the alfalfa their nests hang on,
blackbirds hover directly overhead,
calling.

III

The sickle blade cuts down the nest;
four blackbird chicks ride it, cheeping,
into the grass. The hovering pair flies away.
A buzzard circles.

IV

I walk through willows where more nests hang:
a male hunches his shoulders and hisses,
flaring his red plumage.

V

I walk across a field after mowing blackbird nests;
that grinding sound just behind my head
is a male blackbird flying within an inch,
then darting away.

VI

I sit in the truck drinking coffee,
wondering if science has studied blackbirds.
A hawk bursts from the cottonwood tops; two
blackbirds dart in above him, strike, screech.
He ducks, tries to slash them with his claws.
In relays, from territory to territory,
the blackbirds drive him toward the next field.
Two more rise to meet him.

VII

A Department of Agriculture pamphlet
suggests poisoning blackbirds with Avitrol.
Birds ingesting it react with "distress symptoms and calls."
It may not be used on crops intended for human food.
Blackbirds may be killed when "committing
or about to commit serious damage to agricultural crops."

VIII

I see a newspaper story on a man who
eats blackbirds; they taste, he says,
somewhat like doves. They have no
distinct taste. "Usually" he advises,
"you have to serve blackbirds with martinis."

The Poet Falls in Love with a Cowboy

I'm going home like a section line road,
straight and fast, past empty houses
crouched on hills, past a cat
sniffing the snow wind, coyote tracks
scribbled on a drift, smooth
heifers with blank white faces,
Hereford bulls with icy horns.
Horses, heads bowed, are backed
into the storm. It mounts, plunges
on. The wheels pull the road under me.

A section line road never makes a smooth
womanly curve; it hangs a hard left,
and this wasn't supposed to be your poem.
But you're a man of that land and I can't
keep you out. You're a walking chunk
of the Grand River breaks: bobcats
stalk your skull, grouse nest in your hollows,
coyotes prowl ridges of sinew. If I were
your woman, I'd be rolling north, not south,
finding a straight road to a hidden cow camp.

If I ever see you again, it will be
from the armchair by my own fire, or some
motel room, some airport, some other road
I'll drive, reminding winter that it
owes me mercy.

II

"Our life is frittered away by detail. . . . Simplify, simplify."
—*Henry David Thoreau*

Rankin Ridge: *Only An Ancient Moon*
—for Lawrence

The sun drops below the high tree.
Elk cows the color of grass move
out of the pines,
up the meadows toward a pond.
Dark among the trees the bulls pace,
snort, begin to bugle.
That sound flows across meadows like water,
opening like a piccolo, rising to a keen,
a cry, a wail, a ululation for our night.

The moon lifts, huge, gold, flattened,
pushing to higher air,
becoming small, silver, distant.

The cows graze silent in the growing grass.
The bulls wait at the edge of the trees,
bugling.
The moonlight flickers
at sounds too high for human ears.

Walking Fence

makes spring official,
shouldering a little roll of smooth wire,
fencing pliers in my back pocket.
Cows have been here, looking for holes
in the fence, sliding in gumbo, mud
squeezing between their toes.
The spring is running now—all that
rain. Maybe the dam'll fill up.
                              Cowslips
blooming already, roses on the ledge.
Water has seeped out, two hands full
cupped in the grass, sweet and clear
and cold. Another half mile. Old
John must have set this post—
pure pitch, driven in with a maul.
Still solid, needs a staple.
                              Now
the hill; won't be any problem there
unless the bulls've been fighting.
Tie this spot down with a rock
and I can head home, get those calves
turned in here before noon.
                              Good to know
the fence is up; that's one
job finished.

This Year

The old mother cat greeted spring with senility,
pregnant as usual. She abandoned herself
to affection, rolled over waving her paws,
lost control of her belly. Did she (paw lifted, stalking a bird) suddenly go blank (like grandmother),
pause, breathing in crisp air, listening to meadowlarks, recall frisky tomcats that are whitened bone,
a rabbit she caught when she was young (taste sweet blood)?
Did she forget hunger, thin kittens in the barn?

> Before snow, she was dead.
> I saw a bloody white
> patch on the highway, knew.
> I picked her up gently.
> The ground was frozen. I
> found a cave on the ridge,
> rocked her in with limestone,
> piled high. There snow drifts white
> into the grass, catches
> the eye as she did,
> stalking.

Turtle Dance

The turtles migrate through
Missouri in the spring, slow
claws pulling north. Cars
roll over them, paving dirt
roads in cold blood; earth
is parqueted in crushed green
shell. Nothing halts their slow
dance. I knew a girl who
couldn't stand the crunch;
she'd stop the car, carry them
one by one off the road. She
bought a bicycle finally.
Driving to the store for food
was either too much death
or too much turtle transportation.
That's fifteen years ago.

I know
the turtles still march north.

Nude: 1976

Once a week I pose for artists.
Their pencils trace every wrinkle, sag;
their eyes see only pencils, lines
on paper. They paint a face, half-profile
but not the acres of hay I mowed
to make that shade of brown;
a shoulder with too much muscle
over a fragile, mended bone
which does not show;
nor the hands: corded, scarred,
with swelling veins.
A shadow falls across my breasts,
leaving one nipple in light,
its red mouth trembling.

The shoulder pain is arthritis in the break,
the doctor says. The wrist I smashed
two years ago is still numb. I'm
beginning to realize all this is permanent.

Under the shadow,
under the tan oiled skin,
beneath the white net of ribs,
deeper even than the blood washing
through the heart's ocean
hangs that knowledge (suspended
like an octopus trembling with the tide),
hangs fear.

Sky Ranch: Coming Back

When the schools and cops and courts
give up, they send the boys
to Sky Ranch for one last chance:
put them to work feeding cows,
give them a horse, teach
them to fly. The pilot takes
them up, kicks the stick
over, waits for them to ask
for help.

        Distance takes over:
sixty-five miles northwest of the town
on the river, sixty-five miles
of antelope, eagles, blue sage;
buttes push backs against the sky;
sixty-five miles of gravel road;
the radio station fades, town dims;
horizon wavers green; grass and sky
meet far beyond sight. The ranch is backed
against the river, hands up.

Sometimes it works: a boy
falls into his own soul
and out, like a plane
out of a tailspin. •

Shooting Prairie Dogs

I lie down in the short grass,
sight on a fat brown pup. His
shrill voice pipes over dirt mounds.
He bobs down, up, tail twitching.

                    Shot at
he doesn't run but
sits up, paws folded against
his chest, looks for the overhead whine.

                    Hit, he
jerks, topples, drops. When I kick him,
he rolls over bloody, moving with fleas
like a migrating blanket.

                    Holes he's dug
stand for years, traps for horses
to snap legs in, dens for snakes. Grass
killed by his digging takes years to return,
damage hard to calculate in dollars.
Here I am, who marched behind Martin Luther King,
who stood the taunts behind a sign that read "Silent
Vigil Against the War," ran like everyone else
when the flying wedge of cops hit the quadrangle,
here I am, shooting prairie dogs.

                    I shoot again.
The dog falls in his hole; his heart lies on the edge,
quivering.

Posing

The artist has placed his model
in sharp brown leaves where sun
gilds her open skin, bent
to the camera's eye.

a hunting owl, sound-
less as the orange sun,
rises from the branches,
floats down the gully.

Behind his lens he sees only shape,
flesh dappled with light flung
from the lone cottonwood.
He will seek that shade among his oils.

The man in the darkroom keeps his eye
on her nipple, the curve of her hip,
a gold thigh; doesn't see the owl
develop, hover like a soul
going out or coming back.

Poem for N'de, Too Late

N'de was a Navajo friend,
a potter, killed in a car accident
on the highway that runs
past my house

Take two aspirin
and forget about the Jews; I have problems of my own.
Something in the dark has called my name.

I wake to the cat's purr against my back.
Ping: another jar sealed or the lid
coming off the whole mess at last. Poets are no
better than the rest at reading signs.
Helpless, they write poems to ease pain. Each lover
is good for a line or two; husbands equal sonnets.
Friends vary, but not many get a whole poem, never
while alive. Maybe you're a meadowlark and my words
no longer matter to you. I touch the pot you made
for me with care, afraid it will fall.

Souls of the dead pluck at my hair, twang
each strand, catch at the pencil, try
to finish what they were saying.

                              Hands
that knew clay become clay.

Leaving Fargo: April

The highway's lined with dead black drifts.
Wind tries to push me back north.
Trucks lean like whales into the storm.
Gray trees crawl the horizon;
plowed fields mist, dissolve behind me.
A lean black dog, missing since
December, has emerged from
a roadside ditch to die again
in an April blizzard, winter
resurrected.

In the Dashboard Glow

—for Dan

Like a late night radio station
your signals are beginning to fade.
I keep twiddling the dial,
watching the black highway rush
up along the yellow line.
                                        Eyes
gleam at the roadside. Dead animals thump
under the tires. The lights do not
penetrate.
               Each time I pass you on the dial
I hum a few bars: you live with an artist; she
made a quilt for your water bed; you went
dancing with two high school girls.
                                    I keep
driving. Static intervenes, then a Baptist
preacher who says we're all going to die anyway.
                                            It's

getting harder to hear your tune, though
stations seem to be few in this dark plain.

Uncle

He sips coffee
thick hands wrapped around the cup.
"This generation ain't got no corner on violence."
His sunburned hands, cracked and broken, clench into fists.
"You'd be surprised how many fellas
turned up in their own wells
in the Dirty Thirties."

The drought was less severe, he says,
here where ranchers did not tear the sod with plows.
Most families had enough to eat.
His battered hands fixed fences,
drove the teams swathing hay,
paid out worn bills for the land of those who left.

Now they call him a land baron.
"Quitters," he says. "They gave up.
But someone had to stay—
and that took guts. Men like that
had hot tempers, and did
their own law-making."

III

For poetry makes nothing happen: it survives
In the valley of its saying where executives
Would never want to tamper; it flows south
From ranches of isolation and the busy griefs,
Raw towns that we believe and die in.

—W. H. Auden

Midnight in Missouri

The radio says, "Fifty degrees tomorrow."
But I know that windsound, that nighthowl
clear from the Dakotas, across the Badlands,
prairie creeks, hunting grounds, down across Kansas stubble,
swoosh across the rivers, flatlands, through Missouri's little woods
around my house, still screeching.

How many coyote cries, wolf voices, joined to make that sound?
Spruces whip, wind scours granite rock faces,
pine needles whistle along rock trails,
deer pause, hides twitching, hair blown up straight.
How many mountain lions breathe in that clear keen,
pace along a rock ledge, crouch, flick tail, spring?
Ghosts rise out of prairies where they fell alone,
lay in the sun and rain before the wolves came
and the buzzards circled.

The screams go on within their dusty brains,
ride the wind to mine.

Homesteading in Dakota

It was a typical prairie homestead:
a hundred sixty dusty acres
with not one tree.
Mr. Fisher put up a soddy for his wife, five kids,
and dug a well by hand the first month.
The kids and the woman worked the winch
after the well got below ten feet.
                              He cut logs
in the hills ten miles away for a solid barn,
log-roofed. Once they were settled he went
to the mines in Deadwood, seventy miles away,
for winter cash.
                    She stayed in the soddy,
milked the cow, dug out a little garden,
struggling with the sod laced together by buffalo grass
roots. Now and then she'd stop for breath, shade
her eyes, look at the horizon line
drawn smooth against the sun.

Mr. Fisher—she called him that—
came home when he could,
once or twice a month all summer. Neighbors
helped her catch the cow, fight fire, sit up
when the youngest child died.
                              Once
he got a late start, rode in at midnight.
Fumbling at the low door, he heard struggle inside.
The kids were all awake, pale blank faces
hanging in the dark.
                    When he pushed aside
the curtain to the double bunk
he saw the window open,
a white-legged form running in the moonlight,
his wife's screaming face.
He shot once out the window, missed;
shot her and didn't.

The neighbors said Black Douglas, on the next claim,
walked for a month like he had cactus in his feet.
The kids grew up wild as coyotes.

                              He never went to trial.
He'd done the best he could;
not his fault the dark spoiled his aim the first time.

Haying: A Four-Part Definition

I

When I was fourteen, my father bought a new John Deere 420
for me to drive. I'm thirty-four.
                              Some summers I've missed:
away at other jobs, married, teaching.
                              But I'm home for now.
For the twentieth spring he hitches up the mower,
mows the big yard, stops to sharpen the sickles, straighten
sections, grease zerks.
                    Impatient, he begins before he's ready,
plunges in. When he's made the first land
he stops the tractor, grins, says "I usually drive it in third"
(so do I, I growl for the twentieth year)
                              pours himself some coffee.
I mow around the field in diminishing concentric squares
trying to write a poem about haying.

I I

On the first round: alfalfa's purple smell.
On the third: redwing blackbirds fly up, screeching.
On the fourth: the cupped nest swings
from three plants; *on the fifth:* four chicks,
openmouthed, ride the nest down to die.
On the sixth: I remember the first time. They cheeped
while I carried the nest off the field. Two redwings
fluttered where it had stood. They never went near it;
a buzzard did. *On the tenth:* damp heat induces sleep.
On the twelfth: I watch the sickle slashing.
On the thirteenth: remember a story. A neighbor caught
his pants leg in the power takeoff. When his sons saw
the circling tractor he was a bloody lump, baseball-size.
On the fourteenth: calculate the temperature at
one hundred ten. The first hour ends.
On the twenty-eighth round: an eagle circles up the grove,
pursued by blackbirds. I think of the poem again:
seeking words for the heat, the pain between my shoulder blades,
the sweat bee stinging under my arm. For fierce hot time.
On the fortieth: I think of water. *On the forty-second:*
the sickle hits a fawn; his bleat pierces the tractor's chug

36

like cold water on a dusty throat. He lurches off.
There's no way to see them in the deep grass,
no way to miss. Still, we never tell my mother.
I begin to lose track, listening for loose bolts,
but around sixty my father finishes hitching up the rake,
waves me in for coffee. The second hour ends.

III

hay 1. n. Grass or other plants such as clover or alfalfa,
cut and dried for fodder. Slang. A trifling amount of money.
Used only in negative phrases, especially in "that ain't hay."

IV

Today I mowed ten acres of hay, laid
twenty tons of alfalfa down, raked
it into windrows for my father to stack
this afternoon. Tomorrow he'll gesture
to the two stacks and say, "Well,
we've started haying." In a month
the two of us will put up eighty tons;
by August perhaps one hundred ten.
Hay for the cattle against winter, pitched
out in the snow for their slow chewing, snow
blowing among the stems, drifting on their backs.

Hospital Talk

   —*for Harold*

The tide of visitors washes
just to the end of the bed.
We crash against the silence,
whitecapped with our own fear,
sit or stand looking at his face—
not the flat sheet where
his right leg was.

We say, "This is a nice room,
a better view than the other."
"You look good; better than yesterday."

He says, "I'm gonna have to sell
most of my cows. But I'll buy more,
once I can get around again.
Looks like I'll get them storm windows
puttied and painted, finally."

"Who brought these roses?"
"Is the food good?"

"I've been layin' here thinking,
I believe I can rig the truck so I can drive.
I ain't got the tractor figured out yet,
or the horse.
But I've been working on it in my head
nights when the dark piles up
around this bed like
all that water over Moses."

Exits

I notice footprints on the wing;
rain spatters the windscreen, sliding back.
Clouds are piled like dirty sheets
outside a motel laundry room.
The plane's shadow glides across a snowy field.
You pause beside the car, looking up.
Perhaps you wave.
You are not the same man I left last time.
But I'm going anyway, a one-way ticket
in my purse, carryon luggage stuffed
under the seat in front of me, seatbelt
securely fastened. The "No Smoking" sign is on.
                                                  I know
how to release the oxygen masks if I can't breathe,
where all the exits are,
how to leave my own footprints
on the wing. I know at thirty-five thousand feet
none of this will matter.
                         The silver scythe
of the propeller cuts into the clouds. We rise
into the sun.

Lamp Lighting

At eight, I lived with my grandmother. The lamps
were my evening chore: after I got the eggs,
while the last hen was still catching grasshoppers by the stone step. When the sun
dropped behind the top tree I was inside. The lamp was filled in the morning; gold
pungent kerosene waited. I'd lift the chimney off,
set it on the crocheted cloth, turn the wick
up a little, strike the match, keeping my eye on the wick,
gently turn the knob. The wick slid down,
left flame dancing along the brass edge.
With two fingers (for fewer prints) I'd place
the chimney lightly on the lamp,
                              hold my breath
for the tricky part; if the flame flared up
and sooted the chimney, I had to get a polish rag
and begin again. When the flame fluttered,
began to glow, I'd sit back in the old oak chair,
let the gold light seep into my soul.
                              Behind
the wood stove, over the brass bedstead, unknown
faces hung on the wall, waiting
in the shadows for the light to dim.

Cyllene

*Cyllene: Another name for Artemis
and her sacred tree, the fir;
Birth-goddess, Queen of the Druids,
"the curved Queen, mother of the
tree calender."—Graves, The White Goddess*

I brought home a knotted root
anonymously burled with dirt.
It lay on my porch shrouded in snow
while I worked behind the walls.
Forgetting, I shoveled it away;
summer buried it in grass.
I raked it in with the leaves,
stuck it upright
in a crack between the boards;
went on working.

Spring rains washed it clean,
annoying me with their drumming.
Summer storms polished it,
howling just outside my window.
One autumn day I saw
it had become a woman.
Hooded like a monk—
a nun—a witch—she stood,
hands hidden in wide sleeves.

I drink my coffee slowly at dawn,
watching the rain;
she broods beside me.
At night we gaze, listening,
into the spruce; the owl
hoots at the moon.

I am beginning to talk to her,
to hear.

Telegram Announcing the Death of my Father

I

"Regret to inform you death
this country Robert Bovard. Stop.
Please contact this office
for instructions. Stop."
Next of kin. I last saw him twenty years ago.
I was five. He was drunk.
I feared his face on every wino
but how would I have known?
Mother sobs on the telephone.
Her letter says, "Blue Hawaii.
Sweet Leilani. The Song is Ended.
I shed all my tears long ago."

II

So I sat, telegram in hand,
arrangements made, wondering if
I was supposed to cry. Stop.
The ashes of a man I never knew
were scattered over hills I've never seen.
Surely that's all the yellow message meant.
It's only that night-nibbling mouse
that wakes me tonight, ten
years later, each telegraphic word
gnawed into my brain. Stop.

John Neihardt

Without the eyes you might mistake him for
a tree root, flung from earth by flood some years
ago. The storms have raged, the torrents' roar
receded, borne the soft wood with his tears
and left the hard. The skin, like water wind-
blown, wrinkles over bone, and soft white hair
springs up like drying grassblades, clean and thin,
sun-bright. The nostrils, like a spearhead, flare;
cracked lips like rivulets in bark close tight.
Weeds tangled grow above the hollows for
his eyes—histories are in his eyes, alight
with noon sky prairie blue, where eagles soar.
And from these eyes all he has seen will come—
gnarled shaman writing to a midnight drum.

Dreaming of the Goddess

Waking up to write poems
is dangerous business.
Poems lose their form
under the moon,
change their names,
leave town after dark.
Poems have no family life;
they slip around at midnight
disturbing the nest of sleep.

Waking up to follow them
is often a prelude to madness—
I read somewhere
schizophrenia can be controlled
by attention to diet.
Perhaps that's the answer
for post-midnight poems:
a bit less coffee at dinner,
no wine or lettuce.

Half-dreaming I may follow a poem
to the waning of the world.
Who knows where it goes then?
They wax so quickly I cannot follow,
alter their meters,
assume new identities,
abscond.

Like old lovers, poems are
full of accusations,
fail to satisfy completely.
Like trains at three a.m.
they violate sleep,
privacy,
whistle through the bedroom
in the dark.

Poems pierce my rest,
leaving behind moon-eyed changelings
to confront me in daylight.

This Is

a day to be pleased with small
clean places. The wash basin glitters
white; the mirror reflects my
face, clean and pale. The kitchen
smells of cooking beef, onions,
carrots. I busy myself
with hot water, white suds. On
the rough brown board, the knife blade
waits, glowing.
                    Leaves brush the window.
I stay in, mop the floors, stare
at the red picture frame
around a prairie scene,
polish the lamp.
                    Everywhere the plains
crawl toward me. I suck
them in, slice off neat
rounds, simmer them all day
in the black pot, steam rising
into the still air of small rooms.

At suppertime I lift the lid,
let out a ferocious storm.
A thunderhead rumbles in the bedroom,
lightning flashes among the plates.

I feed.
          Left in the pot: bones.
I throw them out the door
for coyotes, buzzards, grass.

The Buffalo at Midnight

I prefer midnight walks. There's less to see.
All matter casts its forward shadow.
Walking in the dark, under the trees, I tired.
The ground was damp; a large dark rock lay by the path.
"I'll sit on that." I sat.
                    The rock snorted,
shook himself, became a buffalo.
Somewhat out of breath two hundred yards away
I paused to reconsider.

A buffalo may weigh a ton,
stand six foot at the shoulder, be nine feet long,
covered with coarse brown hair, smell
like a ton of angry meat. Mane heavy with night
he lies beside the path, moonlight on the blades
of his horns.

Wherever I walk now,
I become a nerve end, seeking the shape
of whatever lies ahead. Sometimes,
like birds twittering toward sleep, signals
are faint. But I know the buffalo waits.

IV

"After all anyone is as their land and air is. Anybody is as the sky is low or high, the air heavy or clear and anybody is as there is wind or no wind there. It is that which makes them and the arts they make and the work they do and the way they eat and the way they drink and the way they learn and everything."

—Gertrude Stein,
An American and France

"We are the children of our landscape; it dictates behavior and even thought in the measure to which we are responsive to it."

—Lawrence G. Durrell,
Justine

Elegy on a Dead Cow

She hunched her back against the north wind,
searched out a little grass every winter.
She tried to get up one last time, meet it on her feet.
Legs tucked under her she lies dead in thigh-deep mud.
Her brown bucolic eye is glazed, her hip bones draped
with shrinking hide, her sides mud-smeared where we worked
to lift her free. She was too weak, finally, to pull herself
out of the muck. Her lower teeth were gone; she didn't get enough
of the feed we've pitched for sixty days of unremitting snow
and wind.

Fifteen springs she's birthed a calf,
licked him to life, lifting him clear of the grass
with her rough tongue. Fifteen hot June days she's marched
to summer pasture, the calf's head against her side;
grazed, fed her calf, protected him and brought him home
to sell in fall, growing another in her womb.

Now she's
a problem she never was in life: stuck in mud too deep
for any truck, and frozen solid. We find thirty feet
of log chain, drag her to the boneyard to join her sisters.
Coyotes will feast tonight, howling her praises.
We shake our heads and give her funeral oration,
summing up seventeen cold winters, seventeen springs:
"She was a good old cow."

Hands

The words won't come right from my hands
in spring. The fields are full
of baby calves, tufts of hay, bawling cows.
My brain is full—but words won't come.
Sometimes when I'm in the truck,
leading heifers to spring grass, I find a stub
of pencil, tear a piece from a cake sack,
and make notes, listening to the curlews'
wolf whistle. A barb tore that knuckle,
when I shut a gate without my gloves. The blood
blister came when someone slammed a gate
on the branding table; I tore the fingernail
fixing a flat. The poems are in the scars,
and in what I recall of all this, when
my hands are too battered to do it any more.

Instead of a pencil, my hands,
knotted like old wood, grip a pitchfork,
blister on the handles of a tiller. Slick
with milk and slobber, they hold a calf,
push the cow's teat into his mouth,
feel his sharp teeth cut my fingers—
another scar. My hands pour cake
for the yearlings, seed for the garden
to feed my family.

My hands become my husband's, weathering
into this job he chose by choosing me; my father's,
cracked and aged, still strong as when
he held me on my first horse. All night,
while the rest of my body sleeps, my hands
will weave some pattern I do not recognize:
waving to blackbirds and meadowlarks,
skinning a dead calf, picking hay seeds from my hair
and underwear, building fires. Deftly, they butcher
a chicken with skill my brain does not recall.
Maybe they are no longer mine but grandmother's,
back from the grave with knowledge in their bones
and sinews, hands scarred as the earth they came from
and to which they have returned.

When my grandmother was dying, when
the body and brain were nearly still
for the first time in eighty years, she snatched
the tubes from her arms. At the end,
her hands wove the air, setting the table,
feeding farmhands, sewing patches. Her hands kept
weaving the air,
weaving the strands
she took with her
into the dark.

Scrubbing Parsnips in January

There's a modern sink inside the door,
but I always scrub the old way:
with the hose, outside.
The sun shines and it's forty degrees.

Icy water fans over my hands.
I scrub the clinging earth from white,
stalky roots, their legs splayed
like a man's.
                    My mother washes them
outside to keep the dirt
out of the plumbing.

I have other reasons—
the strong earth smell,
the weak winter sun on my back,
chill wind and cold water, those white
limbs open, a thin trail of blood
where my topping knife slipped
and cut my finger.
                    The rich blood threads
between two roots and blends with the clear
water, follows it down into the earth
for next year's crop.

Calving Time

A living calf,
instructed by mother and instinct,
hides like a rabbit
behind two blades of grass.
Eyes roll as I walk past
but he knows he's safe
from me, and from the coyotes.
He's invisible. From a distance,
he is a rock, a bush,
a yucca plant. He's
part of the wildness,
part of the earth.

A dead calf
needs no disguises.
He's alone, exposed,
no options—stark black
or red in melting snow
and greening grass.
His eyes are dusty.
His mother waits awhile,
moves off to graze.
He's part of the wildness,
becoming rock, bush,
yucca plant;
becoming earth.

Butchering the Crippled Heifer

First:

aim the pistol at her ear. Stand close.
She chews slowly, eyes closed. Fire.
She drops. Kicks. Sighs.
Cut her throat and stand back.
Blood bubbles and steams.

Then:

wrap chain around each ankle.
spread the back legs with a singletree.
The tractor growls, lifting;
the carcass sways.

Next:

drive the knife point in,
open the belly like tearing cloth,
the blade just under the skin.
Cut around the empty udder.
Don't puncture the stomach.
Sheathe the knife and reach in.
Wrap your bare arms around the slick guts.
Press your face against warm flesh.
Find the ridge of backbone; tear the
membranes loose. Hold the anus shut;
pull hard until the great blue stomach bag
spills into the tub at your feet.
Jerk the windpipe loose with a sucking moan,
her last sound.

Straighten.

Breathe blood-scent, clean digested grass.
Plunge one arm into the tub, cut loose the heart,
and squeeze the last clots out; slice the liver
away from the green gall, put it all in cool water.
Eat fresh liver and onions for supper,
baked heart tomorrow.

Finally:

> Cut off the head and feet,
> haul them and the guts to the pasture:
> coyotes will feast tonight.

Then:

> pull the skin taught with one hand,
> slice the spider web of tissue with care.
> Save the tail for soup.
> Drape the hide on the fence.

Let her hang:

> Sheet-wrapped, through three cool October days,
> while leaves yellow and
> coyotes howl thanksgiving.

Cut her up:

> bring one quarter at a time to the kitchen table.
> Toss bones into the big soup kettle
> to simmer, the marrow sliding out. Chunk
> scraps, pack them in canning jars.
> Cut thick red steaks, wrap them in white paper,
> labeled for the freezer.

Make meat:

> worship at a bloody altar, knives singing praises
> for the heifer's health, for flesh she made
> of hay pitched at forty below zero last winter.
> Your hands are red with her blood,
> slick with her fat.

You know

> where your next meal is coming from.

Planting Peas

It's not spring yet, but I can't
wait anymore. I get the hoe,
pull back the snow from the old
furrows, expose the rich dark earth.
I bare my hand and dole out shriveled peas,
one by one.

                   I see my grandmother's hand,
doing just this, dropping peas
into gray gumbo that clings like clay.
This moist earth is rich and dark
as chocolate cake.

                 Her hands cradle
baby chicks; she finds kittens in the loft
and hands them down to me, safe beside
the ladder leading up to darkness.
                            I miss
her smile, her blue eyes, her biscuits and gravy,
but mostly her hands.
                 I push a pea into the earth,
feel her hands pushing me back. She'll come in May,
she says, in long straight rows,
dancing in light green dresses.

Hang Gliding

Strap on wings,
step off a mountain
into the wind,
follow it up, circling.
It looks so easy—just look
for a seam in the sky.

Nighthawks (the Indians called them
thunderbirds) have the same courage:
they front the storm, hang among hailstones,
fly straight into the pounding rain.

It's not so much technique
as attitude.
                You know that.
You plan to live again as an eagle,
sinews stretched to the wind; that speck
climbing circles up the face of a thunderhead
will be you some day.

Waiting, I'll fly into the sun, weave
a net of words under the wind,
cling to the storm's eye
far from your lee.

One April Day
—for Lawrence

You pointed out a single lilac shoot beside
a rain-pooled rock. I found another
between two gray dripping pines,
a sparkling rose among chokecherry branches.

                              You said,
"In twenty years there will be a cloud of lilacs
and roses all around this clearing."

                              I could see
them, blooming in that place and time
around your feet. From all your seeds
and shoots, a woven wall of blossoms.

Putting words on paper, crossing out,
crumpling pages in this motel room,
I think of twenty years without you.

You'll be in your clearing, gathering blooms.
I won't be.

                    Someone where I am
may find this love I seed to stiff white pages
(this rainy day) still lilac fresh.

The Last Word

The hen, not quite beheaded, flopped,
splashing my hands with blood;
a dull axe only wounds. We packed
the hens in canning jars, set them
to cook. You sent me away alone.

Crows unfurled their wings
like black silk flags against the dawn
as I drove from your place to my own.

Now, coffee steams in my yellow cup.
A jar of honey catches light,
sweetpeas nod, kerosene in the lamp waits
for evening, the smell of simple food.
In a wooden bowl are two red apples, three
potatoes, one crackling onion, a fresh
brown egg.
            I say to you: one warm brown egg
is stronger than your fear.

Saying Goodbye

takes a long time. I've made
fruitcakes for everyone I know, shirts
for men I don't care much
about (but none for you), crocheted pot-
holders, baked bread, doughnuts,
fed the birds, dipped candles, mended jeans,
darned socks, cleaned house—twice.

                                        I say
you weren't gentle enough, never touched
my hand just in passing,
smoothed my hair. Perhaps the next man (there's
always another man) will. I baked
my love for you in loaves of bread, put
it like garlic in jars
of pickles, sharp as wild grape jam, rich
brown soup tureened in white.
I thought there would be more: mounds of clean
blue shirts, morning coffee,
supper waiting on the oak table by
the west windows.
                        But these
are all: that bread, those jars, like silent
mouths opening, closing in
the still dark cellar.

60

Helicopter Crash

　　　　　—for M.

I have not borne a child,
I refused that sacrifice
of blood and gaping pain.
You and I were children together.
When you walked down that wedding aisle
already bent backward with your burden,
I flinched from the terrible knowledge in your eyes.

My losses are all vicarious;
confronting blank paper, I try to understand.
You were forgiven
when you brought him forth.

Your mother tells me you did not cry
after the crash that blew his world apart.
You searched that field for his pilot's wings.
You walked that field day after day,
brought home a shred of uniform, bits of bone.

A mother shakes her son's finger bones
in her closed hand,
flings them out on the table
to read her sentence.
His fate has been read,
the hand folded.

Settlers

—for Charles, Feb. 29, 1864
and for John, July 8, 1909

They came from England, Ireland, Germany, Sweden—
from lands that held twelve generations' bones.
Where boundaries cramped and eldest sons inherited,
younger sons walked bravely off to Stockholm, London,
bought steerage tickets, carried one small bag (all they
possessed, including socks and muffler, knit
by sisters never to be seen again), endured
the harbor stench, the heaving sea, the weary months.
They stared at Liberty, and pondered stern advice:
"Go West, young man, and vote Republican."
Learning, they worked repaying uncles' loans
for tickets to their freedom. Set loose from
bondage to the land at last—old Europe, the soft
fat lands of Iowa—they headed West.
("Go West, young man, and vote. . .") No voting yet,
only struggling six-horse teams that dragged reluctant
wagons past the Badlands to the Hills, claims selected
with memories of boundaries cramped, of land
that held the bones of generations.
They settled uneasily at first, stared at miles
of undulating grass, seeking neighbors, seeking
even the smoke of enemy fires, sought
trees and roofs and villages; sought in vain.

One by one, the earth touched them;
they touched the earth, stretched
to crumble clods, to smell the soil.
They met the land, made it neighbor, friend,
respected enemy; partner, brother, father, wife—
a home, a land to hold the generations' bones.

Milliron Ranch

For years we've driven this dusty trail
taking our cows to summer pasture.
When I first saw the milliron,
I was a child on a fat mare
beside my father's dancing gelding.
He told me the story:
stout Swede families came west together,
his father among them,
claimed adjoining lands.

They were a couple, the man blond and slender
like his wife and four of the sons,
and blind.
The hired man had black hair, a heavy build—
and so did the other three sons.
In time more dark children were born,
the husband died.
The wife and hired man ran the place.
The daughter grew strange;
rumor said she dug a tunnel to the granary,
where she'd hide when visitors came.

They're all gone now, but not far—
in the cemetery their headstones lie in a row.
The hired man isn't there.
None of the children ever married.
The place was sold when the last one died.
But they left their mark.

On the hill above the house, a long low slope,
they left a monument sixty feet high.
My father says it was the spring chore
filling the wagon with shovels.
Heavy work, so they made it light by giving it a purpose,
marking their brand on the hillside.
Long, dry years they labored, with little money,
but they left a monument still green after fifty years
in the only thing they ever had in excess: cow manure.

Apologies to Frost's Neighbor

I hate to disagree, but
good fences don't make good neighbors—
at least not out here, where we're
talking barbed wire and pitch posts
instead of stone.

My hands are bleeding,
my temper's black and blue
after a day fixing fence
so my neighbor's cows can be kept out
of my winter grass.
We have unwritten laws:
standing on your own land, the fence
to your right is yours to fix;
on the other side, your neighbor does the same.
The first one to put cows into a pasture
looks over all the fence, and fixes it well enough
so the cattle can't get out.

                       This neighbor
never does, never has. I can recall pounding every
steel post in this fence,
tell when I tightened every strand.
It's a good fence,
but we're not exactly friends.

This year, it's critical.
Grass on his side is almost gone;
around my ankles, tall and green.
It's my loss when his cattle get in,
eating a week's feed in a day. So I'm here,
Sunday morning, fixing fence and grumbling.
If my neighbor were here,
we could reason together,
tighten wires until they sang hymns,
worship upright posts.

Medicine Rock Rodeo

The bleachers are crowded, folks
sit on cars in the sun, shade sunburned faces
with hats or hands, share a cold beer
with strangers. Ida asks about Milly's new
grandchild in a patch of shade
beside the hot dog stand. Kids sticky with pop
and cotton candy punch each
other behind the chutes. In the chute, a lean,
brown-eyed man jerks his bent hat
down, tenses his arm, grins and mutters, "Outside."

Late in the dusty day, an
Oglala boy, whiskey-brave, rides a buffalo—
for thirty feet. While he rolls
in the dust, the buffalo collects snowfence
on his horns, scatters the crowd,
and disappears like smoke into the prairie.
On the fence or smoking beside the chutes, the men
squint across the dusty miles
and wait.

Coring Apples

Today I'm preparing apples for the freezer—
ones my mother picked off the ground around a neighbor's tree.
"Too good to waste," she said, handing me a bucket full.
I've got a hand-cranked machine that peels, cores and slices
in one swift turn. Peels spiral down on the table top,
juice drips, sweet red slices fall into the bowl.

Mother tried it once, says it wastes too much.
She prefers bending over the sink for hours,
carefully paring. I've done fifty pounds
in an hour or so; she'll be days finishing hers.
I'll go on to other jobs.
Daughters always go on to other things;
probably she knows that.

I pull off another core, and drop it in the bucket.
At the sink, she finishes slicing, then nibbles
the last scraps of flesh from the core with her *own* teeth,
she reminds me, until not a drop of sweetness is left. Perhaps
she smiles.

Yesterday she called as I was finishing breakfast.
"I'm not going to church today," she said. "I'm going
to make a lemon pie instead." Given the quality
of her pies, that's a religious act.
I never go to church, except on Easter, my annual gift
to her; instead I'm writing a poem.

Drying Onions

They hung in the cellar's dark all winter
untouched by wind and snow white as they are,
until long green shoots reached for light.
You helped me slice them; crackling
brown skins thin as dragonfly wings covered the floor.

Sweet bitter fruits of the earth—
spread on racks to dry, they became
more part of us than we knew or wanted.
Our eyes began to burn. Our clothes took on the taint.
When we made love, your tongue and mine, this mound
of flesh and that, all flavors
disappeared in onion.
                         All flesh is onion,
all sweat and juice part of us, fruit of our love.

Outside, the snow has melted, crusted,
sagged toward the earth. We hack through it, peel back
layer after layer, searching for the white heart,
for earth warm enough to take our seed.

Happy Birthday

When I was five
I learned about running away.
I heard train wheels clacking in the dark.
My mother cried while I slept.

At nine, I had visions of horses.
Blaze was fat and slow.
I dreamed her swift.

At twelve, I learned country schoolyards
aren't ruled by brains. Tired of running,
I socked a nose and found friendship
through violence.

When I was sixteen
I realized my breasts would be smaller,
my hands larger, than I had hoped;
my hair would never be waist-length
or black. But I still learned to say "No,"

At seventeen, I learned boys don't date
girls who live thirty miles from town.
At eighteen, I learned college girls
with cars have friends even when they say "No."

At twenty-one, I discovered rape.
At twenty-three, I married; heard
about open marriages at twenty-six,
at thirty discovered divorce may not be fatal.
I was much better at "No"
but not always
at the right time.

At thirty-five, I found three black hairs
on my chin and clipped them off.
"No! No! No!"

At thirty -six I understood
I'd never have children.
At forty, I resolved
never to spend another birthday
on an island
with people who like to fish.

On my forty-first birthday
I dug two latrines and visited
my Mormon relatives. They had no beer.
They loved the knife in my belt.
"No," I said gently.

Today I'm 42.

How to Find Me

Turn
the radio up, find Willie Nelson.
Follow straight black Highway 79
to Hermosa, past the pond
where we skated in winter. (I collided
with Kiki, snapping off her front tooth.)

Pass
the pond, the town, unless you need gas.
(Ignore the red brick school where I learned fractions.)
If you need beer, buy it at the store on the corner
(since 1979). As you pull back onto the highway
you'll see the cemetery on the hill. (My father
goes there on Memorial Day. He says he speaks
with the dead, considers his future.)

Cross
Battle Creek, pass the highway leading
to the Black Hills, buffalo, pines. Pass the left turn
to my uncle's house. (He'll be in his wheelchair,
or in his truck checking cows. Losing one leg
didn't slow him down much.)

Pass
empty storefronts (where the town was before
the railroad changed everyone's plans). Keep on.
Admire gentle curves and tawny hills, notice
empty ranches, homestead sites marked by one tree,
a collapsed cellar. You won't be able to tell
where a jet crashed. (Helpless, we watched two men burn,
screaming.)

Ignore
the hard straight line of road to the missile silo
(never armed). Imagine ten thousand acres blackened
by fire set by the train. The track parallels the road.
You're almost there.

Top
the next hill. You'll see a shy gray roof
hunkered behind a hill. Take the next left.
Wind through my parents' yard—wave, please—open
and shut two gates so the cattle won't get out,
and pull into the yard. (From the porch we watch
coyotes gulp mice whole.)
                    Have a beer. (Let's talk
poetry.)

Seven Lessons on the Grass

I

I walk across the hills at sunset,
Looking at the grass: red grass,
buffalo grass, brome identified
by the "M" on each leaf. Cheat grass waves
silver needles in the dying light, lovely as rain
but deadly, packing the cows' throats so they can't breathe.
Some settler brought it here, thinking it would help
cover the dusty hills of this new land.

II

Grasses are the most highly developed form
of plant life on earth. Grass can grow
anywhere: salt marsh, desert dune.
Under this windy prairie, buffalo grass roots
plunge and tangle, searching for water.

III

Our business is turning grass to beef
to feed the world. We know
we'll feed the grass in turn.
All flesh is grass.

IV

In spring the greenest crescents
mark winter's deepest drifts.
Grass remembers snow.

V

In winter, wind shapes drifts
to the curve of grass beneath.
Snow remembers grass.

VI

Spring rain has no color save blue
stolen from the sky, green from the grass.
Rain remembers sky and grass.

VII

Walking, I watch the shifting shape
of sun on grass. I lie down, hidden. Grass covers me.
Flesh remembers grass.

V

"The use of traveling is to regulate imagination by reality, and instead of thinking how things may be, to see them as they are."

—Samuel Johnson

"To travel hopefully is a better thing than to arrive."

—Robert Louis Stevenson

"For my part, I travel not to go anywhere, but to go. I travel for travel's sake. The great affair is to move."

—Robert Louis Stevenson

"The road is life."

—Jack Kerouac

Roadkills and the I Ching

The Traveller:

> I'm travelling again, down
> what the cowboy radio station
> calls that lonesome highway.

The Long Enduring:

> I've heard the same Paul Harvey Show,
> the same sad country songs,
> six times. I try not to look
> at the edge of the road.

Darkening of the Light:

> I read my destiny
> in an I Ching hexagram
> of flattened corpses.

The Abyss:

> In the ditch
> a deer's dead eyes
> give back the night's confusion.

Loss:

> Ropes of flesh
> mark the headlight's edge.

Gathering Together:

> Vultures circle
> black threats
> against the blue.

Abundance:

> None of us
> will grow hungry.

Repose:

> A dead skunk is curled
> under blooming sunflowers.
> They still face the light.

Elegance:

> A wing, uplighted
> still, flutters
> in the wind of passing cars.

Scattering:

> When we're together,
> my husband's big gentle hands
> lift the birds
> out of danger.

Nourishment:

> A lean coyote tugs
> on a deer's leg,
> drags it toward a den,
> hungry pups.

The Small Get By:

> A dog killed yesterday
> ripples
> as maggots feed.

Willing Submission:

> At last I know
> where I'm really
> going.

Driving into a Storm

Last night we burned feed sacks
emptied over the long cold. Falling
snow melted on our cheeks, clicked
on the sacks piled behind us.
You stood in your long blue coat,
a red bandana around the gray hat,
watched for sparks in the grass,
in the haystacks. Flaming sheets
of paper rose, swirled in the black smoke,
flew off southeast like crows.

Today my big hands grip
the steering wheel, knuckles scarred.
The plain gold ring is already scratched,
framed by two new calluses.
I'm racing down this road
into the snow. I sing, drink
coffee, think of the job,
ignore the clouds dropping low,
lower.

You've given me so many gifts
and now one more: yourself
in your blue coat, flames
at your feet, standing against
the dark
rolling clouds.

Down the Highway: Your Tax Dollars at Work

I travel a lot, can't afford to fly. So I load my poems,
three notebooks, a sleeping bag, coats, coffee, sunflower seeds,
a pistol, a few clothes and 347 books in my orange pickup
and head down the highway. I see a lot of live animals,
drive over dead ones, and write poems.
I see many things I do not understand.

In Pennsylvania, I saw the sun rise over a huge
lavender barn with red hex signs painted on one side,
and a dead Holstein cow lying in front.

In Rapid City, South Dakota, I saw a militant Indian leader,
often photographed with a rifle, jogging along the highway
in a black and silver jumpsuit. His braids and bearclaw necklace
flopped from shoulder to silver shoulder.

Near Custer, South Dakota I saw a red Corvette backed
into a turnoff at dawn. On the other side of the fence,
in a warm half-circle, lay six Hereford cows,
chewing their cud, batting their long eyelashes,
hoping it would wake up.

In a rest area in Montana, I saw,
scrawled on the bathroom wall,
"Sept. 15, 1982, Charley with a kilo of Panama Gold."
"Sept. 16: Charley: *Which way are you going?*"

One sunset, I rounded a bend on a gravel road
in western South Dakota and saw a dinosaur, knee deep in alfalfa,
head raised. Usually, signs announce concrete dinosaurs
in this state, but none appeared. I speeded up,
just in case.

In Columbia, Missouri, I saw a lumber wagon
pulled by an ancient mule, driven by a gnarled black Methuselah.
I swerved, slowed. No other driver even glanced his way,
causing me to wonder. Maybe no one sees
any of these sights but me.

That's all I needed. From now on I'll keep these sights to myself, and suggest you do the same. I don't want to know about your favorite restaurant in Tulsa, called the Terminal Cafe. I don't care to speculate on why teenagers in northern South Dakota all drive pickups with rifle racks mounted on the rear window, or think about the hairy, upright creatures leaving man-like tracks around Eagle-Butte.

They're all mysteries to me, and they can stay that way.

Interstate 90

For two hundred torturous miles I have guided a rattling green
Honda along the Interstate, considering implications of the
various permutations of farms I have been passing, contemplating
history, and seeing no single other car, no vehicle of any kind.
I've been alone, perambulating in a westerly direction.

Then—fast—I meet a green Ford, two cattletrucksloaded,
a Kenworthhaulinglogs, a blackCorvette, a yellowCougar
and a furnituretruck, twocampers and a pickup pullingaboat,
huddled together, bumper-to-bumper.

What are they afraid of?
The buffalo are gone or corralled,
The Indians generally peaceable.
They're gone
and I'm all alone in the rolling yellow prairie,
headed west toward Kadoka where I seem to remember
seeing a tree.

Overhead, two buzzards circle, circle,
twisting wrinkled necks, casting one yellow eye,
then the other, upon me.
When they eat a dead calf,
they dip their hooked beaks first
into the soft brown eyeball.

For Pat, Who Wasn't Home

The buffalo over the door
of the Last Chance Saloon
is still dead.

The green river's whitecapped under a stone-gray sky,
the empty gaze of the concrete horse. All the hills
lean toward the river, spilling trees.
Coffee is still a nickel,
but I couldn't get you on the telephone.

When I drove this road for the first time,
leaving home for college at the other end
of a short state, I could rely on the coffee
and sour cream raisin pie.

College changed us all; we grew up a little,
fell in and out of love, made some friends,
many of whom are now dead.
My first love's smile died with him in Viet Nam,
on his forty-eighth mission.
My best friend died with her husband and unborn baby
on a highway joining this one a few miles east.

Today, in the rain, coffee is still a nickel,
the pie is fresh, the raisins fat,
the river is green.
                    You elude me,
and the buffalo's eyes are dusty.

Why I'm Wearing Red Lipstick

When you came home with grass stains
on your knees
and said you fell down,
I took off the lipstick.

When you weren't home for lunch or supper or bed
and said you were writing a poem,
I washed off the eyeshadow.

When you said sleeping with her
was to get a job
I stopped using perfume.

When you went to Europe alone
I ran away, through the desert,
to the ocean.
My body went back to you.
My mind remained,
listening to the chattering pebbles
stirred by the sea.

Today my body and mind and I
all packed our bags,
put on red lipstick,
and left your town,
looking for another desert,
a wider ocean.

Showering With a Grapefruit Rind

Mother always kept lemon and grapefruit rinds
tucked beside the sink.
When she finished the dishes,
she'd look out the window, rubbing the skins
over her cracked fingers and elbows
before going on to the next job.

When I was nine, I thought discarded citrus rinds
were her whole beauty secret; that if I
collected them I'd be beautiful too.
Sometimes I waited until she'd
put them in the garbage barrel.
I hid them in my room
among my socks, rubbing them on my face at night
when I remembered. She'd smell them,
feel them scuttle under her hand
when she put clean socks in my drawer,
shriek, and throw them out.

Now she's eighty-one,
I know beauty is not that easy.
Hers has more to do with laugh lines
in her fine skin, smile wrinkles.
She refused to let a dentist pull her teeth,
still drives her car to church.

I eat a grapefruit,
knowing I'll stand in a hot shower
rubbing its shriveled rind
on my cracked heels and fingers,
inhaling the sour, clean scent
imagining skin as soft as hers.

I Followed You

down the narrow beige ship's halls,
said goodbye carefully,
then walked the dark pier-cave alone
stepping on my tears.

In Lincoln Tunnel, white tile and lightbulbs
smothered a singer. I made
one circle like a lonely moth,
then plunged between traffic lanes
into a green-gold corridor toward home.

Overhead ducks flew, irritatingly in unison;
the barns along the road wore fresh-painted hex signs.
I looked for omens: a house roof
sagging green with moss,
the moon, curling like a leaf or the Mona Lisa smile.
Somewhere, at dawn, I saw a lavender barn.

Flying Over the Badlands

From above, I can trace the course of the old river,
twisting through the land. The water disappears.
The bed turns to grass, trees, farmhouse, barns.
I think of lying in bed in that house on dark nights.
You must feel the drum of water, prehistoric swimmers.

A plated claw reaches through a window,
takes an apple from the table.
Teeth clash on a corner of the roof.
Tyrannosaurus Rex lifts a tractor in one tiny paw.
You stir in sleep, cling to one another's unshelled flesh.

Comes dawn: you wake, stretch,
stand on the porch making a yellow arc to the lilac.
("How many times have I told you . . . ?"
"Hush.")

          There's only a plane, high,
passing over; but the land's
uneasy.

Trans-World Airlines

—for Bill, who died

I

"If a Boeing 737
flying at 35,000 feet
were to run out of fuel
(it has never happened)
the plane could glide nicely
some 100 miles to a safe landing
passing over many large airports,"
said the brochure in the seat pocket.

II

We were friends once, and more.
Bill used to explain to me why
my husband couldn't stay home.
His letter was the first
in several years, and short:
"Three things: I love you,
I have cancer, please write."

III

"An airplane doesn't know
whether it has engines
or not.
It only knows airspeed,
and when you have enough airspeed
air becomes a heavy liquid.
An airplane is a boat
floating on air."

IV

Bill, you had more airspeed
than any man ever knew.
With all those Three Dog Night records
played full volume,
All that lip-numbing chili for fuel,
you ought to glide
a long way.

86

I'm six miles up; the pilot says
it's fifty-one below zero outside.
Presumably the airplane
unaware whether or not it has engines
will continue to float on frigid air.
Below, someone has fenced squares,
measured off allotments of space.
From here, the fences disappear
and the old shape of the land
surges up,
lapping at the edges of the sky.

Sky Ranch: The Poet Leaving

> Sky Ranch, a juvenile detention center for
> adolescent boys, is located in the northwest
> corner of South Dakota. Established by a
> priest, it offered flying lessons as part of the
> boys' therapy (hence its name) until the priest
> was killed in a plane crash.

Snowing again. A line of cows winds
through trees to the river.
I stop on the hill's top to look.
Two horses, tails in the wind, lean over the fence.
The little mare, heavy with her first colt,
whickers.
          The hangar door is closed.
Maybe forever. Sunrise glows
on Capitol Rock. Fog

lies along the river, coiled among
the buildings. Someone in a red jacket leaves
the dorm, moves along the walk, going somewhere.

Yesterday one of the boys wrote, "I heard cops
holler and death fell short."
The ranch lies in the river's curve; from here
the ends of the curve point to this hill.

I can get in the truck and go anywhere,
but still wonder about the red jacket
and the fog, still see the ranch eddy in the river
and the branches whirling, caught
in the roots along the bank.

The Blind Corral

Along the highway to Canyon de Chelly
four Navajo boys drive a galloping
horse herd: blacks, sorrels, paints.
Colts canter, nosing their
mothers' flanks, unaware
of corrals, trucks,
saddles, cold bits,
bridles.

Other horses graze hilltops,
unconscious of grace. The wind
billows fine tails, ripples
shining manes. Horses doze
in the sun, race their own shadows,
never looking at fences.

Down the halls of each school
in the land, young girls caracole
and prance. Their long clean hair brushes
shoulders. Faces are open as meadows,
eyes clear as creeks. Fearless, they buy
eye shadow, rouge for false blushes
over fine bones. They ring eyes with color,
force firm breasts higher
into wire cups.

Advice to Jockeys and Others

—for Bill Shoemaker and Ferdinand

Everyone's talking odds, from the plush
owners in their boxes to the threadbare
gamblers down along the track. Talking fast
track, slow track, records, speed.
But the odds don't matter to the horse
or jockey. It's all in the running,
in knowing how to save yourself,
in the finish.
                        Don't worry
if you're dead last at the first turn,
if the camera's eye has lost you,
seeing only the horses in the lead.
You have time to make your move.
(But—just so you'll know—the horse
millions of people are cheering now
will come in eleventh.)
                        Ahead of you,
haunches bunch and stretch,
tails wave, silks gleam. All you can see
are backs and backsides streaming with sweat.
A sweaty rear end indicates effort, but not
necessarily success.
                        Keep running smooth,
long burnished legs gathering up the track,
pushing it behind. Stay on the rail.

When the finish line is in sight, begin
your move, easing along the rail while
everyone watches the lead horses.   Join
the front-runners, looking like a calvary charge.
A touch of the whip—just a reminder—
and you're out of the pack.
                        Cross the finish line
first, where the odds—
remember the odds?—
were 37 to 1
against you.

(In the 1986 Kentucky Derby, Ferdinand, ridden brilliantly by 54-
year-old Bill Shoemaker, exploded from last place to first against
heavy odds.)

She Drives a Pickup Wearing Pink Shoes
                    —for Kathy

We rattled out of Bozeman at sunrise:
you and I and the yellow truck;
left a black cowboy hat and a silver bullet
in the dust, crossing the line before the first snow.
Once we parked the pickup by the Snake and floated on.
But we had to come back: she honked
so lonely from the bank.
                                    Snow lay
on the tent at dawn, so we fled south,
to Virgin country, canyons so still
they echoed thought, dry sandy heat,
and deer in the salt cedars.
                                    The pickup wandered up
and down the trails all night, shining her headlights
under every rock, looking for a ringtail cat.
In Kanab, Utah (eighth healthiest city
in the country) she nosed out an Italian place,
but mostly we cooked on the blue hissing flare
of the Coleman.
                        Old spider women drinking martinis hung
over Grand Canyon, weaving webs. After dark
all three of us escaped,
honking wildly, into the aspens on the Kaibab.
Yellow pickup rutted across the res,
waving at every red Navajo truck. At last
we crawled up the trail to Walpi, looked
on blue corn and silver secrets;
flew into a turquoise sky.

Tapestry

—*for Meridel Le Sueur*

She stretches, sighs, begins untying knots,
loosening the threads
that bound her to this day,
seeking the strands
knotted over the door
to sleep.
                In the darkness,
the rumpled velvet hills are stitched
with silver threads of grass.

Ripe grain and rough brown silo walls
carpet the earth, a tapestry ancient as Europe's finest.
This mat was not woven by the tender white
fingers of virgins, but by the scarred, broken
hands of farm wives. It was created, warp and woof,
of their blood and bones.

They planted children in the earth,
to tie the weaving to the loom.
Plows ripped the seams apart;
patiently, they stitched them up again.

Their weaving blanketed the earth,
supple and strong.
                        Then one and another of the shuttles
stopped; the tired old hands lay still,
were planted in the earth they patched and tended,
made sacred by their work, their burial.

Their children moved on; the towns closed in.
Deserted farms sag and sway:
dropped threads, loosened knots.
Tornadoes spin destruction
that will never be repaired.

                        Above the worn out land
birds swoop like phantom hands,
weaving the clouds.

Not Flying Alone

The old man rises
to the boarding call, rolls
his suitcase on squeaky wheels, hugs
his daughter, shakes
hands with his son-in-law, kisses
his grandchildren goodbye.
As he turns away, his death leaps
from his shoulder, slips
into his shirt pocket.

I am sitting behind him on the plane,
sipping gin. His death leers
at me over the seat, bares
pointed teeth, curls
around the old man's neck,
purring.

Letter Home

I've been thinking of the summer pasture. When I come home next week, I'll go with you over there every day of this fourth summer of drought, six miles through the dust and grasshoppers and a hundred degrees of sun. The neighbors' cattle have leaned through the fence, broken it down.

I've been thinking how we'll pound fence posts into dry earth to tighten the wire. We'll slowly straighten our backs to look toward the Badlands, making blue mirages under the distance.

Thinking how dry the summer pasture is, dugouts all cracked mud in July. Thinking of the seven arching cottonwoods scattered down the draw, the only shade for miles in the glaring noon.

Thinking of Silas Lester's old spring to water cows and us: the pipe we stuck into the flow, the round metal tank under it, walls thick with moss. The water is clear and sweet from the pipe; the dipper hangs on the post, clattering in a hot wind. The water will taste of earth and roots of buffalo grass. I'll take off my shirt, dip it in the water, wring it out and put it back on.

We'll find a cottonwood the cows aren't using for shade, the tall one, near the spring. The green leaves will curl in the heat and the pool of shade will waver around the big rough trunk. I'll sit backed between cottonwood thighs. The sound of the leaves will brush the dust from my thoughts.

Here in this blank motel room far from you, I can feel water drumming under the tree's bark, the earth's heartbeat. I sit tucked between the giant surface roots as if I were wrapped in you. I wait for the owl to glide from the leaves. Perhaps I'll sleep, leaning back against the throbbing trunk in my cool, damp shirt.

You are the spring. You are the tree.

VI

"I thank you for your voices, thank you,
Your most sweet voices."
—William Shakespeare

"out of all sound except the distant speaking of the
voices I sometimes hear a moment before sleep . . ."
—Dylan Thomas

"The people's voice is odd,
It is, and is not, the voice of God."
—Alexander Pope

First Night Alone on the Ranch

The only bootprints in the snow are mine.
The dog you never liked trots at my heels.
The horse looks wary as I pitch his hay;
from here the windows are goldlit,
reflecting on the snow,
but it's only sunset.
The cats are silent mounds.
They are always alone in the night,
their children and mates transient.

I wash the single bowl and cup,
sit by the fire with a book—
remembering how I resented dishes for five,
loud laughter when I wanted to read.
Television tells me that families have husbands,
children, smiling mothers doing the wash.

My family is darkness
before the flickering fire,
the cow calving in the barn.

Fahrenheit

Water freezes
at thirty-two degrees above zero.
Milk freezes
at thirty degrees above zero.
Olive oil freezes
(why would anyone care?)
at thirty-six degrees above zero.
Wine freezes
(mine never even gets chilled)
at twenty-nine degrees above zero.
Blood freezes
(ice clinking in my veins)
regardless of temperature
on January days
when ground and sky
are white and empty.

Up at Sunrise

At 6:30 on a December morning
the sun is one red coal
glowing in the ash-gray plain.
Nothing moves—except a coyote,
ducking into the draw,
me and the blue horse.
The cows are still bedded down,
chewing, steam rising at both ends.

At last the light divides
hill shadow and bright frost.
A Mack with its lights on
rumbles past, dusty
as the snow.
The driver waves.
The country belongs to me.

Clara: In the Post Office

I keep telling you, I'm not a feminist.
I grew up an only child on a ranch,
so I drove tractors, learned to ride.
When the truck wouldn't start, I went to town
for parts. The man behind the counter
told me I couldn't rebuild a carburetor.
I could: every carburetor on the place. That's
necessity, not feminism.
                              I learned to do the books
after my husband left me and the debts
and the children. I shoveled snow and pitched hay
when the hired man didn't come to work.
I learned how to pull a calf
when the vet was too busy. As I thought,
the cow did most of it herself; they've been
birthing alone for ten thousand years. Does
that make them feminists?
                              It's not
that I don't like men; I love them—when I can.
But I've stopped counting on them
to change my flats or open my doors.
That's not feminism; that's just good sense.

Handbook to Ranching

　　　　—for my father

Don't spend any money.

To conserve energy,
when a pickup is not moving ahead
shut the motor off.
Starters and batteries are cheaper
than gasoline these days.
Waste not, want not.

Don't keep horses in the corrals.
If there's snow on the ground
a horse can get by in a pasture without water.

Get the calves fed and watered before noon.
John Lindsay used to say
if he didn't get the work done in the morning,
he might as well go fishing the rest of the day.

Don't take chances. Don't get caught in a storm.
A cow can take more weather than you can.

Don't scatter thistles or cheat grass;
stack them in one pile and burn it.

Scatter hay in little bunches so each cow
or yearling can have one to itself;
they won't eat hay
after they lay on it.

Don't waste feed; know how much
you're feeding to every animal.
A penny saved is a penny earned.
Never call a veterinarian if you can avoid it.

You can never tell what a bobtail cow will do.

Rancher Roulette

It's no trick to get killed ranching.
You might get a foot caught
in a stirrup when your horse bucks, get dragged
to death; that's what happened to my half brother.
He was riding that ridge to the south there;
his wife found him, after the storm.

Or tip the tractor over on a slope. Or forget
to turn off the power takeoff, and get your pants leg caught.
That happened to a neighbor, back in the forties.
By the time his kids saw the tractor circling,
he wasn't any bigger than a baseball.
Just wound him right around it.

Or you could get bit by a rattler, fixing fence.
I killed one with my shoe once, clean forgot
that left my foot sort of vulnerable.
Knew a fella ended up in a dam, drowned;
folks said he must have fell off his horse
and hit his head, but he was courting the daughter of a man
who didn't like him much.

A horse can kick you in the head;
you can get hit by a bull or stomped
by a cow that just calved. I got thrown from my horse
one time—well, more than that—but this one time
I was knocked out, and when I woke up
my head was between two rocks.
If I'd hit either one,
my head would have popped like a watermelon.

Knew a guy fell off the windmill once—
he was fixing it and the wind come up. Jammed his hips
up somewhere around his ears. I damn near drowned
trying to get a rope under a cow stuck in a mudhole.
She thrashed around and pushed me under.
I finally lassoed her head and drug her out that way.
She died anyway; broke her back.

Freezing to death would be easy. After I fell
in the creek chopping ice I damn near died
before I could get fifty feet to the pickup.
It makes a person wonder if there ain't some other way
to make a living. I heard the other day lightning
struck a fella's place on his fifty-fourth birthday,
killed fifty-four cows standing under a tree.

He said, "I hope I don't live to be a hundred;
I can't afford it."

Ralph Jones: On Borrowing

"Neither a borrower or a lender be,"
my old dad used to say. And he was right,
for reasons he never even thought of.
If you lend, your wire cutters will come back—
if they come back at all—with rusty blades.
The shovel handle will be cracked, the pickup
out of gas, with a suspicious whine
under the hood.

If you borrow, you'll feel the brakes
mush underfoot—like stepping in a fresh cow pie—
just as you round the bend by the big cottonwood tree.
Or the dog will discover a craving to bury
dehorning cutters.
                    The sun won't shine
on borrowers or lenders either. Better,
like rain, to do without until you can
get it yourself. Honestly.

Auction

The house stands empty, all the crowded rooms
strewn in the yard, as if exploded
by a bomb, dead center. In one corner
of the empty living room, Gladys rocks
by a window, where she can watch
the auctioneer sell her life, the crowd bid,
turn the things she treasured into antiques.
Two old women sit with her; others drift
in: "That set of china brought seventy-five bucks!"
"I should sell my Fostoria," one of them says,
"It's been in storage for twenty years; I thought
the kids would want it." She shrugs.

Fifty miles away, Asa lies in a white bed
wrapped in tubes like a kitten in a basket of yarn.
He didn't know Gladys yesterday, doesn't know
about the sale. His shop was the best; Asa could
fix anything, make new parts out of junk. When
his knees went, he built a little cart to drive
to his shop, and to get the mail. Out back
piles of iron loomed like pyramids, and he knew
exactly where to find whatever he needed.
Maybe in his mind he's in the shop, among the tools,
cans of carburetors, stacks of hubcabs, still fixing
broken sickles, turning a piece of iron
into an invention.
                    The auctioneer says it again:
"Asa made this," and his brother-in-law,
who never made a thing, cringes, then smiles.
Asa won't be making anything now.
                              "And it's a . . .
what is it, boys?" the auctioneer has to ask.

It doesn't matter; the folks will buy. Some
of them are thinking of Asa when they bid.

Alice Johnson: Matriarch

      —for Meridel Le Sueur

See these fine white lines carved into my belly?
I won that decoration learning how to bear a child.
After that, I learned to nurse him,
as these splayed nipples show, to raise him, teach him
strength. These lines on my face represent my graduation:
when I lost him to the gun of another boy,
son of another mother.

This crooked wrist is my medal for learning one does not strike
a horse that's doing her best. These white hairs shine
as a badge of all that I have learned.
Let them glow and multiply as I learn.
Let me bow my head to none but women
with more wrinkled faces,
more white hairs.

These broken hands have comforted a dying friend,
pulled a shaft of pain from the heart; were torn
as I climbed the barbed wire barriers of ignorance,
broke my fingernails on the brick walls of patriarchy.

Young women, do not take pride
in the blank page of your smooth skin.
You have much to learn.
Don't color around those wide eyes; save your energy
for seeing. Your breasts are virgins, proud, intact.
When they droop like mine, what will you have learned?

Young women, listen!
You're praying to the wrong gods;
sacrificing only hairspray and face paint.
The Goddess calls for blood and pain.

106

New Year's Eve: After Leaving My Husband

Flute notes fall,
splinter—icicles.
Behind a lighted window
someone lonely
notes
year's passing.

When afternoon was sinking
into dark, a child laughed
outside, then a man.
They passed my window
sliding in the snow.

Grim-faced
an old man cycled the other way
balancing his head
and the hat on it,
pedalling
between sweeping flakes.

Now the black dog
runs from behind
a white starched curtain,
ducks under a window frame,
disappears without a sound
behind the other curtain.
He didn't seem to care
about the flute.

Perhaps if I lie down with care
I shall hear a new tune
on the ceiling.

Before I Met You

The bluegrass band was
picking under storm clouds: wind
rushed toward the sunset.

Guitars thundered
in black rolling clouds; a lightning
banjo flashed; fiddles
trembled, sweet and high among
the trees. Then: mandolins rained
and he was gone.

Here the plain
with its single cottonwood
lay in the sun all day
like a supple girl with a gem
in her navel.

His letter said, "The wind is chill here,
like when the snow goes off
in February, and water stands around roots,
and about dark a front moves
coldly down."

Now I Know Grouse

Know the legs muscled flat
against fleshless backs;
know heavy flight.
I pull feathers, snap ribs.
Blood from the thick dark breasts
stains my fingers;
a shot clinks in the sink.

I know too why you hunt them:
walking tense beside you through the trees,
all of us in line, scanning the gray grass,
ears strained for the clucking rush,
the shotgun butt, the blast,
the tumble of feathers.
Grouse hide well in the grass,
bundles of meat and feathers,
quivering with fear.

I know your squint at the sun,
how you carry a shotgun
like a pistol in one hand,
know your broad shoulders
between rows of corn,
know how you fire without aiming,
eyes on the gray thing you love and kill;
know your brown eyes, crinkled from looking
at the sun, horizons, bottomland;
know the blue firelights in your black beard,
its crispness to my fingers.

I know how you love and kill.

Child's Play

Like a child on a flying saucer,
spinning, cold plunging in my ears,
I whirl away from you.
                         Where am I going?
Backwards, now. Away, surely.
I have one look at you:
brown eyes, a scarlet slash of scarf.
The disc spins. You
and I
are gone.

Yet in the end, will the world fling itself
snow over sky and you meet me
in warmth beneath the snow-chilled slope?

The saucer scrapes rock, slows, stops.
Brushing the snow away, I trudge uphill.
The snowfall has begun again.
I cannot see the hill's top.

Priorities: 1898, Upper Yukon

Inspired by The ABC of Mining: A Handbook for Prospectors
by Charles A. Bramble, 1898 (Rand-McNally)

I

The three prime wants are food, clothing and shelter,
and their importance is in the order named . . .

This list should feed
one man for twelve months:

Sugar: 75 pounds
Apples (evaporated): 50 pounds
Salt: 25 pounds
Salt Pork: 212 pounds
Pepper: 1 pound
Condensed Milk: 1 case
Flour: 2 barrels
Candles: 1 box
Matches: 12 boxes
Soap: 1 doz. bars
Tea: 1/2 case
Beans: 200 pounds

II

Ignore the dictates of fashion on the mountainside,
and beneath the pines.
Dress resolves itself into a question
of warmth and comfort.
Cut is of importance
only insomuch as it allows free play
to the limbs;
to the arms in digging,
and to the legs in climbing the stiff side
of a canyon.

For arctic conditons on the upper Yukon
choose an outfit such as the following:

2 heavy knitted undershirts
2 flannel shirts
6 pairs worsted socks
2 pairs overstockings

1 pair miner's boots
1 pair gum boots
2 pairs moccasins
1 suit homespun
1 horsehide jacket
1 pair moleskin trousers
1 broad-brimmed felt hat
1 fur cap
1 Mackinaw overcoat
2 pairs flannel mitts
1 pair fur mitts
1 muffler
1 suit oil slickers
1 pair blankets

In cold weather feet, fingers, and face require the most care.
The first should be stowed into two pairs of wool socks, and
    draw
a long pair of knee-high oversocks over these.
Boots must be replaced by moccasins.
A pair of thick worsted mittens, and a pair of leather mitts outside,
keep the hands warm enough
even at 20 degrees below zero.
At 50 degrees below
put on an extra pair—
or go home until the weather moderates . . .

III

The favorite style of architecture in the wilderness
is neither Doric nor the Gothic nor yet the Renaissance.
It is called the dugout.
A hole in the side of a dry bank,
a few sods or logs for roof,
and there you have it.
A veteran miner goes to earth as easily as a rabbit,
and, like bunny, is never at a loss for an
habitation.

Next to the dugout the log cabin deserves mention . . .
The only drawback to the pre-eminence of the log cabin is
that to make it you must have logs—
just as the cook always insists on pigeons before she makes pigeon
    pie—

and logs are in some districts known only as museum specimens.
Now, the dugout . . . only requires a gravel bank, or
one of those deposits of argilite that the vulgar persist in calling clay;
were it not for this fatal ease of getting, every miner and prospector
would doubtless prefer living in a snug log hut,
there to await in peace, comfort,
and dignity the arrival of the
representative of the "English syndicate" to whom
he is destined to sell his claim . . .

IV

In summer, from June until mid-August,
the mosquito, the black fly and the midge, or sand fly,
make life a burden in the north.
The best remedy for the mosquito and the black fly is
a mixture of tar and olive oil
the consistency of cream
rubbed on all exposed parts of the person.
A dark green veil will also keep the insect pests out
of the eyes, mouth and ears,
and in winter is better than snow goggles to avert blindness.
But, unfortunately, it interferes with the enjoyment of the pipe,
and hence is not in much favor with woodsmen.

V

The existence of the prospector being passed
in regions where the so-called benefits of civilization
have not penetrated,
he is generally a healthy, happy,
hopeful man.

Especially hopeful.

I do not remember ever meeting one
that was not brimful of expectation
and trust in the future.

Perhaps prospectors that grow pessimistic
drop out of the ranks.

113

MacDuff: A Scot in the Country

They call it retirement, but
just marking boundaries is a big job:
four bowls of water a day.
I get up at six, wake
the woman and her cat,
hustle out to my rounds:
woodpile, bonepile, pumphouse,
spruce, bunkhouse. Cats
appear, strange fruit
in the winter trees.
The snow seems deeper here
than in the city: I'm undercoated white.

Hustle, bustle, pee, to the barn,
the junkshed, plowing snow
with my mustache, barking
so she knows I'm on the job.
I keep checking the woman, watch
her drink her coffee, the damned cat
on her lap. When she drives off
in the pickup, I find that one
can climb too. I watch
the rooster strut inside his pen,
exchange snorts with the gray horse,
sit on the porch in the sun,
cleaning my feet, bay
at the neighbors' truck. But
it's not all rest. On Monday,
the neighbors helped her butcher.
I must bury the bones
of a whole steer.

I liked the city, but I've been around,
seen it all: poets, pretty ladies,
hustlers, bright lights. Spent three days
in a bar one time, bumming peanuts.
I enjoyed it all like a big T-bone.
But I'm no pup; it's time
to be here, with no cars,
no sidewalks. In the country, a dog
can mark his bounds
with no one to complain.

Fourteen

I can ride my horse faster than my best
friend Mikkey, and lean far enough off
the side to pick up a handkerchief
from the ground. We've been best friends
since she broke a raw egg over my head
and I punched her in the nose and made
it bleed. She didn't cry.
                    I didn't either
when my horse fell and I broke my wrist.
I picked tarred gravel out of it
for a week before my folks took me
to a doctor; he said
it was broken.
                 I don't have pimples.
I don't like boys. My dad couldn't
whip anyone, but I can whip you.
I'm glad I don't have breasts;
they'd get in the way when I'm up to bat.

I'm not afraid of anything but rattlesnakes,
lightning when I'm on the horse,
my father's rare anger.

It's only on the outside
that I'm 41,
hair going gray,
divorced,
childless.

Tomboy

Boys never make passes
At girls who wear glasses. Ya ya ya.
Boys never make passes
At girls who wear glasses.

When I was eleven, skinny blonde pigtails
waggled like beagle ears, thick glasses
roosted like buzzards on my nose, gum
tangled in my braces. My mother married
a rancher and we moved to the country.
I wanted to be a boy.

Boys had swaggers and zippers in front,
knives bulging their jeans.
Dad gave me a jackknife; I practiced
mumblety peg, and cleaned
my fingernails in public places.
But when it was my turn to bat
during recess I couldn't hit the ball.
I couldn't catch either. Once,
when I was standing too close to home plate,
a boy threw his bat and knocked me out cold.
I came to with a hatred of baseball.

But I still wanted to be a boy.

Two little lovebirds
sitting in a tree
K-I-S-S-
I-N-G

Girls wore dresses every day, painted
their fingernails; instead of baseball,
they sat in the swings, talked
about boys and giggled like geese.
A redhaired girl named Judy wore lipstick
and a padded bra. She swung her butt (a word
Mother slapped me for using), batted
her eyelashes. The other girls followed her
like ducklings. The boys forgot baseball;
spent recess leaning cool against the wall

116

around Judy, spitting authoritatively between
their shoes, putting their arms around Judy.
I hated her, and I still wanted to be a boy.

I scream
you scream
we all sceam
for ice scream

Terry was my friend, the only girl I wanted to be like:
a seventh grader, lean, mean, tough.
She never noticed me, but her sister Kathy
was in my grade. In winter we ice skated
on a dam at recess. Playing Fox and Geese, Kathy
and I collided; my head
knocked out her front tooth.

On sunny days we ate lunch by the stone wall
in the sun. Terry said, "Let me crack my boiled
egg on your head," Grateful to be noticed, I agreed.
It wasn't. As the slimy mess dripped
off my specs, I vowed revenge.

Alle allee
oxen free!

When snow lay deep on the playground,
I caved a snowbank on her head and ran.
She thrashed
then thundered behind me;
I knew
I was going
to die.

I turned, stuck a fist in the air,
eyes closed. Her chin slammed into it,
blood spurted from her nose.

Bam! We were friends. I helped her wash the blood
off her face with snow. Later, I'd stay overnight
with her; we'd go to her church in the morning.
She asked a nun if I would go to heaven or hell.
"She could still go to heaven if she becomes a Catholic,"
the nun said, not looking at me.

We rode our horses in the summer parades, barrel
raced and beat the boys. We raced our horses, never
really knowing which was faster, hers or mine.
When my horse fell and cracked my wrist, I didn't cry.

Liar liar,
pants on fire
liar liar
pants on fire
hanging on a
telephone wire

Then Terry
went off to high school.
The next time I saw her
she was wearing a girdle,
lipstick, nylons.
She got pregnant,
walked down the aisle in white,
smiling with her teeth.

First comes love,
then comes marriage,
then comes Terry
with a baby carriage.

Hannah: Dying in the Hospital

My life was clean: a clean house, the children's clothes sometimes faded but scrubbed in the tubs outside the kitchen door.

Oh I remember the heifer struck by lightning on the hillside one July day. Clean knife strokes cut meat from the bone, packed it into clean hot jars that boiled four hours in the deep kettle on the wood stove. A hundred ten outside. I stoked that range all day and most of the night. Bright jars of canned meat lined the counters on clean dish towels when the others woke up. My brothers and sisters. Mom couldn't manage it all, with eight of us. She cared for the little ones and the garden. I did the rest. The boys kept the wood box full.

When I married it was more of the same. My man didn't seem to have much juice in him, after the twins were born. Just rocked and smoked. Found that job at the vets hospital. I kept the place together selling eggs and butchering chickens for the store.

When the oldest boy could drive the team, we did all right. He took over the farming. The twins were off to school by the time my husband died, but the oldest boy stayed with me.

I was tired by then, before mother came to live with us. She was like a big baby, and I took care of her, kept her clean. Then my daughter came home with her daughter, and got a teaching job, and I had another one to raise.

Lord! the pies and cakes and canned meat I've put in the cellar! Enough to feed an army.

I was ready to go that cold night; breathing was so hard, and my arms were tired. But you had to load me in the car and bring me here, here to tubes in my nose, dried blood around the tubes in my arms.

I'm hooked to this bed like a bee. We used to catch them, and tie a string round them, and fly them around our heads. But I don't fly no more, I just lie here buzzing.

What's that smell?
Antiseptic, but it's not really clean, not like my kitchen, or the death I thought I'd have.

119

Goodbye

This frail April day
we delayed
as long as we could.
On the porch stand two clay mugs,
one orange, one blue: both empty.

VII

"Love consists in this, that two solitudes protect and touch and greet each other."

—Rainer Maria Rilke

"You have to learn to do everything, even to die."

—Gertrude Stein

"Life only demands from you the strength you possess. Only one feat is possible—not to have run away."

—Dag Hammarskjold

Wind

Books on nature seldom mention wind;
they are written behind stoves
—Aldo Leopold, Sand County Almanac

Wind defines the land,
shapes everything outside the window,
screams down the chimney,
whistles through each crack.
Old-timers say the crazy winds
always last three days.

Bunch grass ripples on prairie hills:
a thousand coyotes running for cover.
Hawk settles, clutches stone,
sweeps into the wind,
battling north.

Cows drift south searching for calm,
eddies in the flow.
Horses snort, whirl,
dance on invisible rapids.
Cats face it, sniff passing worlds.

Beside the highway white grins gleam
above tawny grass: flying styrofoam.
Beer cans leer, copulate, filling valleys.
Plastic wraps the barbs.
People blind to coyote
toss garbage out windows
of speeding cars.

The wind will take them all.

You Loved Those City Lights

Just married, we'd driven all day
toward graduate school,
beginning
life together with second-hand
furniture piled U-haul high.
Despite our dirty jeans, old shirts,
you led me to the tallest building in St. Louis.

"We can live it up one night," you said;
held my hand in the elevator,
reminding me I'd never been higher
than the roof of the barn back home.
You strutted into that saloon
as if already wearing
the silk shirt I'd buy for you
later that year, with money from my night job.

You whispered that the lights below the tower
looked like diamonds just out of reach,
talked the band into letting you sing.
Your honey voice flowed over the room.
You calmed me when the waitress snatched
our supper money for her tip.

Clouds tumbled, wind whined; we watched
umbrella-covered tables thirty floors below
topple into the pool. A tiny man
clung to a fence. Arms windmilling,
he slipped into the shallow end;
soggy, climbed the ladder out.

"Like Laurel and Hardy," you said,
snapping your fingers to the jazzy beat.
You pointed out the lights below the bluff.
"Poor folks live there, over the river.
But baby, we're always gonna be up high."

The bar TV flashed tornado warnings.
Black musicians grinned with white teeth.
The drummer claimed his riffs
could make the tower spin.

White men in three-piece suits
pretended the spire swayed;
their shining women shrieked.
Waitresses, round trays aloft,
wheeled drinks faster and faster.

When I stood and pointed, the music ebbed.
Below the bluff, lights spun, dimmed.
A murky vortex swept along the river,
swallowing glitter,
swallowing broken glass,
swallowing light.

Shearing: Wyoming

Passing, I catch one glimpse:
a ranch on a gray hill,
five pickups in the yard,
children running with dogs.
Behind the barn, men in bright shirts
stoop; a corral full of skinny sheep,
very white, bleat and thrash.

                   The road and I rush
on, somewhere. Behind us sheep blat
and freeze; dogs—leaping—hang in air;
children never grow up.

Calvin

Doomed to be short and fat,
he dreamed himself sinewy lover,
Shakespeare of the *Rodeo News*.
Among lean brown men at the chutes
he scrawled bull-riding metaphors.
Cowboys spat just past his Tony Lamas,
jerked their hat brims down.
When a roper said, "Nice story
on that Tucson rodeo," Cal bought cigars,
drinks for the house,
dreamed of headlines.

At night in gray motel rooms,
he spurred the pain sunfishing in his gut,
wrote love sonnets, emptied bottles.
Every five years he mailed
a sheaf of poems with no return address
to a writer he once knew,
gave some to a girl he just met,
sent them off to magazines.

One year he turned up late
for the National Finals.
"Where you been?" the riders asked.
"You missed that last go-round."
That night he told loud, funny stories
from half the rodeos he'd seen,
seduced them into buying drinks for him,
recited poetry until his voice
whispered into silence.

Reading Cal's obituary, one cowboy
shook his head, spat gravely into the dust.
"Dead before the booze wore off,"
he said. "That's something."

Hunter's Moon Madness

Rising
it silvers the hills.
A coyote chants refrain
to a distant pack.
Voices glitter over the black valley.
The night is laced with cries:
nervous killdeer,
warbling frogs.
Silence.
Something hunts
the pond's edge.

The cat paces my windowsill
longing for the night.
But he's old and slow,
his eyesight's dim,
the coyotes might catch him this time.
And yet, why not?
He'd die hunting,
blood burning in the dark,
even his bones consumed.
No hole to dig,
no door shutting him underground.

Night tempts me as well.
Do slender forms dance
through moonlight?
Black wings cover the moon?

I crouch,
shut in with my prey,
dark shapes stalking,
stalking.

Behind Roughlock Falls

An ouzel feeds on the creek bottom,
flies through liquid air;
scales a mossy cliff, curtained
by waterfall.
We stumble through spray,
stand invisible to tourists
at the railing far above.
My toes twine in the sandy floor.
I lean against you
warm inside the sound of water;
smooth shapes shatter, roaring.

In winter a skin of ice
leaves water murmuring
deep within the falls.
When I emerge, dripping,
I look warm as anyone else.
All the way home you do not speak;
blood whispers beneath my skin
inside a cage of ice.

Walking the Dog

—*for Frodo, March 1989*

Walking a dog in the city humbles me;
we're used to acres of prairie privacy.
I pretend to walk for my health, striding up the walk
past clipped lawns, fenced trees, flower beds,
tugging the dog toward the curb.
"He was my husband's dog," I explained as I left the meeting,
as if being true to George's memory
meant nothing more than taking his dog
to mark territory four hundred miles from home.

You've seen us, or a similar pair:
the human studies the sky, historical plaques, treetops,
apparently unaware of and not responsible for
what the dog at the other end of the leash is doing.
The dog plays his part: stares at bicycles,
challenges windowed cats,
barks at children on a merry-go-round.
He lifts his leg as a cardinal
might lift a hand over a crowd of pilgrims,
with immense dignity, a modicum of grace,
and an expression of concentrated rectitude.
He's a short dog, but his eyes
focus on higher things: the heavens, and
flying squirrels which he—and I—
believe to be ghosts of those caught by larger dogs
whose mark he senses when he stands beside a tree.

Without George I'm like a dog,
dangling at the end of a leash
held by someone I hardly know,
looking and sniffing for a familiar tree,
some landmark among fumes from asphalt, exhaust,
and unknown legs. Neither of us could scent
our real home from here.
It's lost behind us
with the man who put our collars on
and whose identity we shared
as we sat beside his campfires.

Back in the car
the dog curls up on his back seat blanket
dreaming of a place where he catches rabbits—
instead of only smelling the ozone of their passage,

where George tosses chunks of fresh venison
over the campfire's coals at night,
and in the morning leads him beside still waters
waiting for a dry fly to land, a trout to rise.
I keep awake, read maps, watch the gas gauge,
try to determine where we go from here.

Waiting

After all the waiting,
empty time wrapped in a paper cocoon,
doctors find a lump
in a breast still childlike
when all the other girls were women.
Pain where I've nursed only joy.
No child, and now too late.

A woman with small cold fingers
maneuvers my body
into warped postures
seeking a machine's verdict,
conjecture at best.

I learn a harsh word
with no motion, no warmth:
fibro-cystic. Give me a metaphor.
This new ruler of my breasts
demands sacrifice: no caffeine.
I acquiesce to its demands,
but there are no guarantees.

I wait for a clear blue image
from the machine's mouth:
the breast as volcano
rises pure above a frail cage of ribs,
too fragile for this weight.

Driving to Chadron, Listening to the News
        —October, 1990

All night a leader twists
in sleepless rest, dreams bullets and blood.

East, a gray November sun
rises shrouded in clouds.

West, behind a dark battalion of hills,
tomorrow's snowstorm blazes with reflected sun.

North, fighter planes disappear into clouds,
their screaming engines splinter air.

South, along the road I travel,
a thousand crows erupt
from the rotting corpse of a roadkilled deer.
Black silk wings unfurl,
blotting out the light.

Following a Cabin Cruiser in a Blizzard

Nose raised to the wind,
I'm headed west on Interstate 90.
No landfall in sight;
I couldn't even see
the last rest area I passed.
Snow thin as spray or blown salt
drizzles across the hood.
The car keeps drifting off course,
pulled and pushed by wind.
My sails are reefed, hatches battened down;
everything loose rattled to rest
when I skidded into the ditch.
On a sunny day I'll sort and stow it back.
For now my goal is somewhere I can't see,
a rocky shore hidden by clouds, wind, fog.

Occasionally a small, fast craft
appears off my port side,
shoots past me into white froth.
The car rocks on wind and asphalt waves.
I think I'm on solid land,
passing small farms with lighted windows
where farmers pace while wives fix dinner.
My eyes see nothing but heaving white.
Prairie folks love ocean metaphors—
long before the first college rose,
some cowboy tanned to leather by the sun
called my country the "sea of grass."
We're desperate for any kind of water.

The bowsprit lifts, points at sky;
waves thump the hull,
crash on trees to starboard.
The flashing light of the truck
hauling the cabin cruiser
becomes a lighthouse,
a buoy warning of deep water.
I'm afraid to stop
the steady engine throb

and step outside—
my foot might find nothing,
my body sink, my lungs fill
with salt sea water,
or blood.

The New Hope City Bank

The hands that hewed these beams are dust,
but I still stand sandstone square
at the end of the block. Though the street
before my brass-bound doors is empty
where once a dozen wagons rolled
full of families come to town to buy,
I'm still here. The hotel across the street
burned down ten years ago; its lot
is weed-grown, bottle-littered, path-slashed.
The livery stable became
a telephone office, then a bar
before its roof fell in after a snow.
They cleared the rubble and it was gone
as if it never was. But I'm still here.

I've seen the church grow old
where Calvin Coolidge heard a long-forgotten sermon.
She's white and pure as ever, virginity intact—
but faded as the spinster who pumps the Sunday organ.
I didn't build this town, but moved in with the railroad.
This vault held money for a hundred farms.
When prices dropped, it held the farms.
(Land is nothing, the deeds are all.)
Those were the days.
But the highway went right past,
the bars closed down, people moved away.
A violin-maker moved in, became justice of the peace,
declared your fine while tightening a string.
After he died, someone boarded up the windows,
took the violins. I stayed.

Fifty years I stood empty, except for mice and flies.
Last year they sealed the crack—sidewalk to sky—
that let in rain and snow, fixed the roof,
washed the windows, put new oak counters
where once sat desks and clerks.
They never found the vault door.
I could tell them who took it away,
but those days are gone.

A woman serves ice cream where the president sat,
looking sternly through his gold-rimmed specs,
and grinned the news, "Foreclosed!"
It's not the same.
That's not a complaint.
I'm still here, solid,
four square at the end of the block.

Visit to Huntington

Blue pipe smoke trapped beams of dust
as we were mesmerized,
suspended by the poetry he spoke.
We felt ourselve akin,
four neighbors in a sunlit room,
communing. Ice cubes clinked
in amber. Reminiscence brought
vignettes: the Orient
with mysteries of brass and horn, dark jade
in twisted gold, the face
of Mexico in beaten copper, chairs
handsewn in creaking hide.
Watusis carved in wood
hurled spears beside scenes daubed in oils somewhere
behind his past. We walked
through nations in our minds, heard lutes and drums,
saw thunder crushing hills,
felt tears of laughter in a way unknown
before his voice. Like gods
we questioned man, progress, fate.
The poet listened.
                        We did not see him go;
his return broke off our talk. Between
huge hands cragged as rock
he held three bowls. Chinese, he said. With care
he moved an ashtray, placed
frail painted bowls on bamboo bar.
He tapped them to produce
three tones, each sweet, translucent, lacquered,
rich as gold and delicate
as lace. He smiled and struck again. Each long
tone rang alone, a song,
remembrance of ten centuries of man.

VIII

"In three words I can sum up everything I've learned about life. It goes on."
> —Robert Frost

"We're all in this alone."
> —Lily Tomlin

"Keep Breathing"
> —Sophie Tucker

"You only live once—but if you work it right, once is *enough*."
> —Joe E. Lewis

Drowning

I

A woman who lies down beside still waters
will dream deep rock-lined pools,
fish swaying to great green rhythms
slower than a tree's heartbeat.
Lying beside rapids, she'll
turn restlessly, spatter quick words,
dream the busy mutter of rocks.

Women who lie down beside water
become water:
bodies swelling like waves,
eyes cool and deep,
hands and tongues slender,
quick and curious as fish.

I I

Words bubble out of my heart,
staining the page: stories at night,
lines while I'm doing dishes.
Dead weights fall from my life.
I float to the surface
bloated with thoughts.

Hyacynth and watercress tangle my hair
trout lip my eyes,
whisper in my decaying ears.

A fisherman casts flies
to lie in the still water
just out of reach
of my fleshless fingers.

Standing Stones: Loch Stemster

This rocky rain-soaked land is Caithness,
identified with the Cat Men
by authorities
who don't mention Cat Women.
With sharpened antlers someone
chipped blocks as tall as I am
from quarries beyond that rise,
chiseled limestone gray with age
and eons from its deep sea birth
into thirty-six massive columns.
Using oxen shoulder blades
they scraped thin soil to bedrock,
hacked a footing,
heaved each stone upright.
Through fifty thousand days like this
the stones have held their course,
scoured by wind, greened by lichen,
crumbling gently in the rain.

Fog swirls within my skirt
as I pace the circle, stone by stone.
Each faceless pillar
stares straight back;
behind me each becomes
a towering woman in a hooded robe
gazing out of time.
Breath condensing in the misty air,
I chant the ancient names:
Annis, Branwen, Brigit, Domnu,
Morgana, Morrigan, Wyrd.
Morgana, Morrigan, Wyrd.

                              Wind
in the colonnade whispers.
Ashes of dead elders
solidify, lift like smoke
from tiny tumbled cairns
at each stone's feet.
Gales sweep the moor,
a battalion of swords solid as flint.

I would worship fire
if I had steel, or tinder,
or anything to burn.
Beside an egg-shaped cairn—
a stone mound enveloping
a womb-shaped chamber—
a fresh circle has been laid
by priestesses I shall never meet.
In three directions the moor is cloaked in heather;
eastward, oceans roar against the coast.
My dead husband's coat, too large,
fills with wind until I can believe
he's inside it with me,
a wraith with warm arms.

The hooded women wait.
My questions are the same as theirs,
resounding down twelve hundred years.
The stones stand firm.
The answers are the same.
The answers are the same.

Dear Suzan

Since coffee talk and promises to write,
the hay has grown, been mowed and stacked.
Hawks are moving south, fighting crows;
the last tomatoes ripen on the window sill.
Your children must be in school.
It's not that I don't remember;
days are short. Often when I plan to write

cold and dark eddy around me
tangling at my throat,
rising from the twisted roots
of dead tomato vines;
frost tonight promises winter soon.
Crisp orange petals tumble at my feet
as ripe black marigold seeds tumble into a jar.
When the earth is frozen outside the window
I'll touch the warmth of summer in stored seed.

Dawn, After Hearing William Stafford

The poet speaks, the river flows;
the river flows, the pheasant
on the other side cough-coughs.
Catnip pokes through leaf layers,
tiny weeds promise. Birds whose
cries I can't identify bubble
in the trees. A mourning dove—
I know that one—hoots.
                                The river bank
is caving off, floodwater rising fast.
A cottonwood branch, dead white,
is stuck deep in the bottom mud; it bobs
against the current, pointing upstream.
An elm tree, roots exposed,
flings itself back onto the bank,
gains a little more time.
Cold rises out of the fields.
The cows are awake, staring
with incurious eyes. The poets are asleep.
I slip away at dawn, away from the flood,
the river flowing bank full;
away from the poet, taking his words along.

Even in sleep the poets hear the birds calling.
The river flows, taking anything it can;
the river flows, bank full.

At the Poetry Festival

Eighteenth reading of the week,
or maybe twenty-third,
I hunched near the top of the auditorium,
glazed eyes trying to focus
on the pit below,
where poets struggled
with nets and tridents to be original.
Some got stuck, others netted.
My mind, I admit, drifted a little.

Around me, students wiggled,
trying to figure out
how this would help their grades.
I hadn't been outside for three days,
smelled flowers, or written a decent line.
I missed my husband,
who wouldn't go to a poetry reading
if they handed out free chocolate.
Someone mentioned "existential plasticity of form"
and "iambic assonance dematerialized its premises."
The air was still and hot,
as were the poets.
I slumped, stretched.
I may have dozed.

A movement cornered my eye
beside my chair,
a tan leg,
gleaming with softly gilded hairs;
a shapely, muscular,
most definitely masculine leg.
I hadn't seen a leg like that since . . .
I couldn't even remember.

What if I stroked it gently,
making all the little hairs stand on end?
What if I grabbed the ankle and dragged
the leg out into the hall?
Outside into the deep grass?

Was the Muse speaking to me
in a new way?
Was She
trying to tell me something?

In a fashion characteristic of my species (poet),
I thought too much.
A gong sounded.
The leg was gone.

No, I didn't turn around.
I didn't watch that leg walk out of there,
or see what it was attached to.

Sometimes,
in long poetry readings,
I shut my eyes
and reach down beside my chair.

The Successful Writer

The poet's words will sear the page like coals
in snow. What he creates will sound of larks
rippling within the hushed dawn
as the coyote bitch relinquishes the night,
assume the shape of plains that sweep to some
remote and instant gasping rise of earth
flung upward, peaked, becoming mountains grouped
in clannish snags around an ice melt lake;
be frail symmetrical success;
taste of honey rolling in the throat;
prickle as do salt grains on the tongue;
sound a plant in darkness where each beast
peers out in terror from his bone-strewn den.

This Poem You're Thinking About Writing

—for 18 Students From Stevens High

This poem doesn't tiptoe
timidly to your side,
slip its soft white
hand into yours,
whisper
in your ear.

This poem leaps at you,
stabs its fangs
into your hand,
hooks ten sharp claws
into your throat
and bellows "LISTEN!"
Your blood
drops steadily
to the floor.

This poem is tired
of pussy-footing
around.
This poem is meaner
than a rattlesnake
tied in a knot,
tougher
than a bull's hide
or a cowboy's rear.

This poem says
"Take off those dark glasses,
quit lying to yourself and
everyone else.
Let's get DOWN to it, baby."
This poem wants a revolution,
a body count.

This poem is yours.
It's waiting
just behind
your eyes.

149

Missing the Chance

In another summit's dusk
I heard her shriek—
reverberating still
in the badlands of my skull.
I want her in my eyes, my soul.
Tongues in my veins call her sister,
mother, grandmother, self.

Inside willow shade
I kneel to drink
strawberry-flavored water
from my cupped hand.
Sunlight flickers. A shape ripples,
leaving one pawprint:
four round toes around a fan.
Water flowing into the muddy mark
spins with my brain; when it stills,
I can whisper: puma, *Felis concolor,*
cougar, panther, mountain lion.

Her track is larger
than my stained hand, spread.
At the edge of sight, water seeps
into another pawprint.
Willows shiver; the stream breathes.
If I look, she'll be there.
If I follow, she'll be here.
Tawny stalker, golden-eyed watcher,
she glows like ruby strawberries
in a green meadow,
like aspen leaves
on the peak at my back.

I cannot pad softly away,
leaving water-filled pawprints.
On the height golden light flares,
vanishes, long tail shaping air.
Silent, I offer strawberries
in scarlet hands.

The Iron Pool at Ojo Caliente

I. The Pool

Step into shimmering emerald,
sunlit by skylight.
Sit on the concrete shelf under water,
peer into the pool's dark end.
Rocks in the shadowed wall
become saurian heads
cemented in stone.
Float closer; the illusion grows.
Smooth oval heads, eyeless, gray-green;
mouths barbed with poisoned teeth.
Does one lizard turn
toward warm pink flesh?
Sound slithers—a hiss,
or water streaming?
Static, they chill.
Swim back to the light.

So what kinda car is your dad buying you?
Mercedes.
So what color Mercedes you gonna get?
Red. Or black.
How come you're not getting a Jag?
Mercedes costs more.

II. The Hot Wrap

Lie on a flannel sheet on a narrow table;
a soft stepping woman
wraps you tight as a mummy
in gray wool blankets, pads away.
Sweat pours down eyelids,
over shoulders and belly, tickles ribs.
Doze to the murmur of water running,
swishing as tubs are cleaned.
Gazpacho, savory as sin, braces the belly.
The chimera's predatory hiss
is almost drowned by water
bubbling.

151

Ironwood Trees: A Painting

—for Lawrence, who owns the land;
George, who cut the pines;
Tom, who painted the scene.

I

Our friend, who owns this forty-acre plot,
plans a memorial to you, a bench
near the aspen grove you saved by cutting pines.
We spent the warm fall days working
together. With the chain saw,
you'd drop and trim a tree, cut it into firebox lengths.
I'd stack wood in the pickup bed,
heap brush too small for fuel into piles
we'd light when snow was deep enough
to keep surrounding trees from catching fire.
You stopped more often than I liked:
to get a fresh chew, tighten chain or sharpen it,
add fuel, or sit in the sunlight
listening to the dog bark at squirrels he couldn't reach.
I'd bring the water jug and lean
against you, thighs and shoulders warm.

While you listened to that silence,
I'd think of winter nights ahead.
I could see us reading or making love
inside the blizzard's core, warmed
by the wood we'd harvested together.
I thought we were only working hard
toward one winter's rest.
I didn't know your life was almost past,
how long I'd live without you.

II

Before I married you, and since you died,
I walk these woods with the man who owns them.
He knows how to keep busy: planting lilacs,
putting signs where hunters would invade
to shoot the deer he feeds with corn in winter.
He has always lived alone.
Often in late afternoon, we walk

152

through aisles of trees,
descend into the cool ravine, dark with shadows.
On the rim above us,
the sun lights one ironwood tree,
leaves us like promises.

The House with Three Blue Windows

Driving north to the retreat, I never see it.
Perhaps it exists only when I go,
reluctantly, down the valley to town.
Each time I am surprised by the blue-trimmed windows
on the second floor.
The center one is taller, wider
than the others.
Above all three, a broad crimson stripe
painted on peach-colored walls
creates the illusion of a bulge,
a bay reaching toward the river.

Three blue windows in a house
with walls of mellow bronze.
Can one who watches through them
see gargoyles in the rocks
across the river, as I did today?
Or does the world before them
acquire a sweeter curve,
remain in perfect round?

A slim, dark girl gets off the school bus,
stands smiling in sunshine
under the blue windows.
Halfway down the road to the house,
three dogs, quivering with pleasure,
wag all over.

This World, and the Last

Across the river
clouds conceal the mesa.
White billows tether each juniper,
tangle in the rippling edges of oak leaves,
snag on a pine tree's branches,
spiral around its trunk.
Of yesterday's sea
only fossils remain, sounding treetops.
There can be no second thoughts.

Creep among plum bushes across a field
without waking the dogs;
step from one stone to another
on the river's bottom.
Hurry between juniper,
cloaked in haze. At the ridge crest
search quickly for the altar stone
that does not recognize itself.
Breathe mist into the caverns of your chest,
dream a rocky headland, sobbing gulls,
waves drumming shoreline in rhythm
with the heart behind your ribs.
One breath, two; it's best not to count.
Breathe. Believe.
            Wake damp, chilled,
to a stone obelisk leaning over heather,
gorse instead of juniper,
fog rolling a pristine ocean.

Traveling Poem

Spring is moving up the river,
swimming hard against the current.
Drain antifreeze; get out roadmaps.
This poem remembers
long adobe houses in flesh tones
hugging earth like nudes of many tribes;
huevos rancheros burning tongues;
deep sky in blue-trimmed windows.
This poem pulls out before dawn, engine idling;
weaves among sleeping buffalo, melting snowbanks,
headlights off until it reaches the highway.

Overhead, stars hang heavy,
but this poem keeps moving,
sees only spinning asphalt,
hot sand walls rising on either side,
rivers curling around its ankles.
This poem arrives at your doorstep
with its thumb out, sandy sleeping bag
over one shoulder, needing a bath.

Give it a sandwich, an oil change,
but don't expect this poem
to stay long.

After the Rain, I See Her Walking

Most days she walks fast,
straight down the center of the road,
two dogs roaming ahead.
Today the mud is slick, ankle-deep.
She climbs the grassy bank,
disappears into the woods above our town.

Straight upslope she strides,
rests leaning into the grade,
goes on. She pushes through gaps
between trees,
seeing each cedar as a miracle.
We locals cut them for fenceposts, firewood.
A ponderosa pine tree three feet thick
lies across her way,
small limbs chopped off for fuel, trunk left to rot.
Turning in a circle, she sees miles
of green tree tops rolling over low hills.
She shrugs, goes on.

When the ground beneath her feet
begins to flatten, she is still in the bushy cedar
mixed with scrub oaks, studded with pine.
She stops under a ponderosa,
leans back against the broken trunk
burst by lightning. Speckled like snakeskin,
it writhes with the force of rain, snow,
wailing wind, and years.
Gold resin trickles down the bark;
fallen branches are grayer
than her mother's hair.

The woman shakes her head, goes on,
staring at the ground,
at feldspar boulders globed like brains.
White quartz veined with salmon
lies among volcanic stone
softened by lichen.
She studies thunder clouds hovering in the west,

gathers lupine seeds, penstemon,
starts to stuff them in a pocket.
Stops, opens her hand. They fly.
She goes on.
A granite boulder, shoulder high,
squats between two pines,
one felled by lightning, charred by fire,
one still flourishing.
The living and the dead.
Lying down on its flat top
she waits for lightning.
If it does not strike,
she will go on.

Alphabetical List of Titles

About the Author

Linda Hasselstrom was born in Texas in 1943, and moved to a South Dakota ranch when she was nine years old. She got her first horse, began exploring the prairie, and started keeping journals and writing a novel. Work in the night staff of a daily newspaper expanded her writing experience while she finished her senior college year and began graduate work. With her first husband she moved to Columbia, Missouri, where she received an M.A. in American Literature from the University of Missouri. In 1971 the couple returned to South Dakota, founding an arts magazine and independent press with the help of the South Dakota Arts Council.

The magazine, *Sunday Clothes,* and Lame Johnny Press operated until 1984. By then, the writer and her publishing business had survived several financial crises, including divorce, and were almost self-supporting. During that year, she published an anthology of South Dakota writers, edited *Journal of a Mountain Man: James Clyman* for Mountain Press of Missoula, Montana, and had her first book of poems published. When she received a fellowship in poetry from the National Endowment for the Arts, she suspended publishing and devoted time not spent on ranch work to writing.

Windbreak: A Woman Rancher on the Northern Plains was written from the diaries she began at age nine and submitted to twenty-four publishers before appearing from Barn Owl Books in Berkeley, California, in 1987. A sequence of essays, *Going Over East: Reflections of a Woman Rancher,* won the first American Writing Award by Fulcrum, Inc., and was published in a hardbound edition during the same year. *Roadkill* was also published in 1987 by Spoon River Poetry Press, which reprinted her first book of poems in 1990.

During 1988 her second husband, George R. Snell, died. Hasselstrom's daily journal of the first calving season after being widowed was featured, with photographs, in the July, 1989, issue of *Life* magazine.

Hassèlstrom was named South Dakota's Author of the Year by the Hall of Fame and received the 1989 Governor's Award for Distinction in Creative Achievement. During the next three years, she published essays on environment and ranching in many magazines, including *Christian Science Monitor, The North American Review, Northern Lights, High Country News,* and *Snowy Egret.* In late 1991, Fulcrum published *Land Circle: Writings Collected From the Land,* essays with poems. Excerpts from the book have appeared in *Reader's Digest, Utne Reader,* and several anthologies and are scheduled for reprint in several college textbooks.

Hasselstrom says, "The work that occupies most of my time—writing and ranching—is complementary; physical and mental labor blend smoothly into a whole. I see my life as a circle: writing about, and laboring on the land of the Great Plains. As I've grown older, keeping my roots in this arid soil has helped me to develop as a writer and as a human being, and to be a responsible rancher. Rodney Nelson (of *Dakota Arts Quarterly*) once said, 'She can deliver a calf and a poem on the same day—after mending a fence.' That statement summarizes the kind of contribution made by many rural people, who choose to be where we are because we love the land, independence, challenges, even the harshness of the prairies. Our experiences are a microcosm of the nation's settlement, and a forecast of the future."

Acknowledgements

I am especially grateful to friends who made me comfortable in their homes while I made two epic tours of the northern Great Plains in spring, 1992, driving nearly three thousand miles. I carried new poems with me, reading some to audiences, and submitting them to the scrutiny of friends who are poets. Thanks especially to Carolyn Bell, to Larry Holland, to Jeff Crandall, and to David Pichaske, whose thoughtful critiques improved this work.

I am honored to wear the 1991 Elkhorn Prize, a trophy belt buckle awarded for poetry by *Nebraska Review* of Wayne, Nebraska, where crowds came for my poetry readings in spite of a classic spring blizzard.

This book reprints the entire contents of *Caught By One Wing* (Julie D. Holcomb, publisher, 1984; reprinted by Spoon River Poetry Press, 1990) and *Roadkill* (Spoon River Poetry Press, 1987). Some of the poems published in *Caught By One Wing* first appeared in the following periodicals: *Country Woman, Black Hills Monthly, South Dakota Review, Shelly's, Jump River Review, Northwoods Journal, Sez, Free Passage, Plains Poetry Journal, Passages North, scratchgravel hills, Northeast, Midwest Quarterly, Womanpoet, Sandhills, Cottonwood Review, The Spirit That Moves Us, A Press, Dakota Arts Quarterly, North Country Anvil, Fine Arts Discovery.*

"Posing" was originally published as a poemcard by Piirto Press, and was among several poems selected for reading on KUSD Radio at the University of South Dakota, Vermillion.

"Sky Ranch: Coming Back" was published in *The Spirit That Moves Us* anthology, 1979.

"Cyllene" appeared in *A Change in Weather: Midwest Women Poets,* Rhiannon Press, 1978.

"When My Father Waters His Trees" appeared in an anthology, *The Midwest,* by *Womanpoet, 1985.*

"This Is" appeared in the *Great Plains Poetry Anthology* from Point Riders Press, 1983.

"Blackbirds" appeared in *The Windflower Home Almanac of Poetry,* Windflower Press, 1980.

Some of the poems published in *Roadkill* first appeared in the following magazines: *Midlands, Bloodroot, Sez, Shelly's, scratchgravel hills, Black Jack, Elkhorn Review, Northwoods Journal, Dakota Arts Quarterly, Green Bowl Review, Dakota West, From Seedbed to Harvest: The American Farmer, Poet's Portfolio, Juxtapose, An American Anthology, Milkweed Chronicle, Plainswoman, Passages North, Chariton Review, American Land Forum, Latuca, Prairie Winds, Midwest Quarterly, North Country Anvil, Wyoming: The Hub of the Wheel, Men and Women: Together and Alone* (1988) and *The Decade Dance* (1991).

Some of the poems printed in *Dakota Bones*, not reprinted from *Caught By One Wing* or *Roadkill*, originally appeared in slightly different form in the following publications:
"Showering with a Grapefruit Rind," *Crone Chronicles*
"Ironwood Trees: A Painting," *Prairie Schooner*
"Shearing: Wyoming," *Northwoods Journal*
"Waiting" and "Drowning," *Swamp Root*
"Walking the Dog," *Nebraska Territory*
"Following a Cabin Cruiser in a Blizzard," *Beyond Borders,* anthology (New Rivers and Turnstone Presses, 1992)
"The New Hope City Bank" as "Hermosa Bank," *Dakota West*
"Dawn, After Hearing William Stafford," *North Dakota Quarterly*
"At the Poetry Festival," *Guadalupe Review*
"This Poem You're Thinking About Writing," *Prairie Winds,* Black Hills Cooperative, Spearfish, South Dakota
"Traveling Poem," "Behind Roughlock Falls," "Missing the Chance," *Prairie Winds*, Dakota Wesleyan University, Mitchell, South Dakota
"Thanksgiving Prayer" in *After the Storm: Poems on the Persian Gulf War,* ed. by Jay Meek and F.D. Reeve, Maisonneave Press, 1992.

166